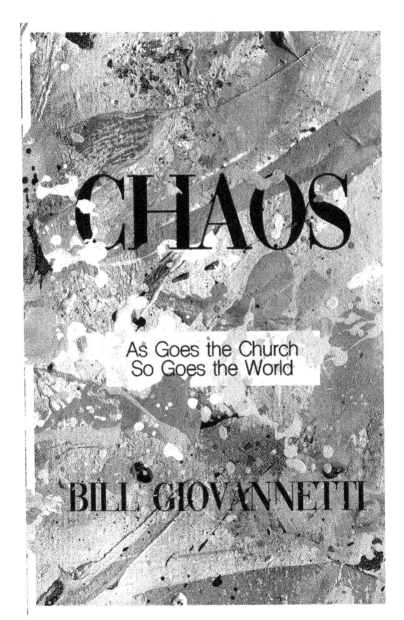

CHAOS

As Goes the Church
So Goes the World

BILL GIOVANNETTI

CHAOS

AS GOES THE CHURCH SO GOES THE WORLD

BILL GIOVANNETTI

ISBN E-book edition: 978-1-946654-23-6

ISBN Print edition: 978-1-946654-22-9

Cover use of the font *Vogue* is licensed under Creative Fabrica B.V.

For additional resources, please visit maxgrace.com.

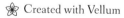 Created with Vellum

CONTENTS

WHAT IS AN EVANGELICAL?

It might be helpful to define a term I use throughout this book: *Evangelical*. To some, the word conjures a cadre of narrow-minded bigots plotting to take over American politics. For others, the word represents the last, best hope of any decency in society, as well as the most faithful custodian of the way of eternal life.

Not to be confused with *evangelism,* or *evangelistic,* which should apply to all branches of Christianity, *evangelicals* represent a specific tribe within the Christian universe.

There are evangelical churches, evangelical denominations, evangelical colleges and universities, publishing houses, ministries, mission organizations, and Christians.

While there is a great deal of diversity in operations and even in some beliefs, evangelicals all share a common theological core.

I will start with the description provided by the National Association of Evangelicals (NAE). Evangelicals are a limb of the Protestant branch of Christianity, with four distinctives:

- *Conversionism*: the belief that lives need to be transformed through a "born-again" experience and a life long process of following Jesus

- *Activism*: the expression and demonstration of the gospel in missionary and social reform efforts
- *Biblicism*: a high regard for and obedience to the Bible as the ultimate authority
- *Crucicentrism*: a stress on the sacrifice of Jesus Christ on the cross as making possible the redemption of humanity[1]

By this standard, count me in. LifeWay Research, in cooperation with the NAE, has simplified these distinctives:

- The Bible is the highest authority for what I believe.
- It is very important for me personally to encourage non-Christians to trust Jesus Christ as their Savior.
- Jesus Christ's death on the cross is the only sacrifice that could remove the penalty of my sin.
- Only those who trust in Jesus Christ alone as their Savior receive God's free gift of eternal salvation.

I would couple these distinctives with the doctrinal statement of the World Evangelical Alliance:
We believe in:

- The Holy Scriptures as originally given by God, divinely inspired, infallible, entirely trustworthy; and the supreme authority in all matters of faith and conduct.
- One God, eternally existent in three persons, Father, Son, and Holy Spirit.
- Our Lord Jesus Christ, God manifest in the flesh, His virgin birth, His sinless human life, His divine miracles, His vicarious and atoning death, His bodily resurrection, His ascension, His mediatorial work, and His Personal return in power and glory.
- The Salvation of lost and sinful man through the

shed blood of the Lord Jesus Christ by faith apart from works, and regeneration by the Holy Spirit.

- The Holy Spirit, by whose indwelling the believer is enabled to live a holy life, to witness and work for the Lord Jesus Christ.
- The Unity of the Spirit of all true believers, the Church, the Body of Christ.
- The Resurrection of both the saved and the lost; they that are saved unto the resurrection of life, they that are lost unto the resurrection of damnation.[2]

These are the people, the churches, and the belief system I have in mind when I use the term *evangelical* in this book. Furthermore, I place myself unabashedly on the conservative and theologically fundamentalist end of the evangelical spectrum.

I'm not suggesting for a minute that genuine Christianity is limited to this evangelical tribe. I am simply saying this is the segment of the church that reared me, and that is making me bite my nails. This is my tribe. These are the people to whom I wish to speak.

---

1. These distinctives are called "Bebbington's Quadrilateral," developed by historian David Bebbington. "What is an Evangelical?" from the National Association of Evangelicals, https://www.nae.net/what-is-an-evangelical/
2. From the website of the World Evangelical Alliance, *Statement of Faith* at https://www.worldea.org/whoweare/statementoffaith, retrieved, April 21, 2019.

FIRE ON THE HORIZON

"DON'T WORRY, HONEY. They'll never let that fire reach our neighborhood." My teenage daughter stood beside me, outside our home, looking at the glowing night sky. The sky shimmered with an orange hue because a fire raged out of control in the national forests just west of our home. That glow had been there for two weeks. For some reason, the smoke on this night was thicker than usual.

Fire season is a way of life in northern California. Government policy simply lets the fires burn. We'd seen it before many times. Maybe we'd grown complacent. After all, we had heard plenty of warnings. The forests were too thick. The undergrowth was out of control. The whole region was crackling dry, and ripe for disaster.

But the warnings fell on deaf ears.

I stepped outside early the next morning to a rain of ash and the strong smell of smoke. We would evacuate our home that day. Little did we know we'd be prohibited from returning for the better part of a month. The Carr Fire turned out to be the most devastating fire in California history, only surpassed weeks later by the deadly Camp Fire.

These fires were the culmination of decades of neglect.

Complacency. Policies that made no sense. Irrational procedures. A toxic indifference to the dangers staring us in the face.

The consequences were catastrophic.

I am writing because the Church has seen the glow on the horizon for thirty years, and ignored it.

The fire is now at our doorstep. Somebody needs to shake us from our slumber.

TRIGGER ALERT

The following book is a rant. Some readers may be triggered. You've been warned. I hope my rant is tempered by a deep commitment to Christ and a lifelong love of the Church.

Nevertheless, the incremental increases in worldliness, the rise of subjectivity and emotionalism, and the epistemological drift in the Church away from the Sacred Scriptures have combined to set evangelicalism on fire.

But the Church acts as if it is situation normal. Smoke is on the horizon, and ash is drifting onto our heads. The Church is in deep trouble. Our roots are smoldering. The freedoms we once enjoyed are scorched. Our Judeo-Christian heritage turns to ash before our very eyes, and our only response is to pen another love song to Jesus.

> Blow the trumpet in Zion, And sound an alarm in My holy mountain! Let all the inhabitants of the land tremble; For the day of the Lord is coming, For it is at hand. (Joel 2:1)

What will it take to wake up the Church? What will it take to shake our complacency? To challenge our irrationality? To rattle our toxic indifference to the dangers staring us in the face? Where is the fire hose to wake us up?

The most likely answer may be severe persecution.

Or pestilence.

Or economic collapse.

Or tyranny.

Please, Lord, no.

Even so, as goes the Church, so goes the world. America today is on the same trajectory as Europe—with Christianity as a dim memory at best, or object of scorn at worst.

God isn't blind.

He sees his own people and their culpable ignorance of him.

Yesterday's prophets warned us, but we turned a deaf ear. Francis Schaeffer predicted *The Great Evangelical Disaster*. C.S. Lewis warned of *The Abolition of Man*. Dorothy Sayers foresaw our "flight from reason and the death of hope." Their dire warnings have come true, but we've been too "busy for Jesus" to notice.

As with most things in life, there's the easy way, and there's the hard way. God sent prophets to summon his people to the easy way – return to the Lord. They stoned the prophets, and in so doing, chose the hard way.

I pray, for my children's sake and their children's sake we don't make the same mistake.

The clock is ticking.

I write as a Christian first, and as a pastor second. I do not claim to be a scholar. Nor do I claim to have all the answers. But, having stood in pulpits for forty years, I can smell the smoke. I hope to God the fires can be quenched. What follows is one feeble man's effort to sound the alarm, and call the Church back to her roots, even as we seek a heaven-sent revival that alone can restore our land.

This book is not yet another call to more committed, more fanatical, or more devoted Christians.

It is, rather, a call to the Church to grow so deep in our knowledge of our God of All Grace, that we rise up to our full stature as joint-heirs with Jesus and as children of a Great King.

It's not too late. Let the Church arise. Let us pack on some Cross-exalting, grace-saturated, Bible-centered, theological muscle. And let us turn, and kick the devil in the gut. May the ear-splitting roar of the Lion of the Tribe of Judah resound throughout our land.

When Jesus came into the region of Caesarea Philippi, He asked His disciples, saying, "Who do men say that I, the Son of Man, am?" So they said, "Some say John the Baptist, some Elijah, and others Jeremiah or one of the prophets." He said to them, "But who do you say that I am?" Simon Peter answered and said, "You are the Christ, the Son of the living God." Jesus answered and said to him, "Blessed are you, Simon Bar-Jonah, for flesh and blood has not revealed this to you, but My Father who is in heaven. And I also say to you that you are Peter, and on this rock I will build My church, and the gates of Hades shall not prevail against it." (Matthew 16:13-18)

How MANY PARTS can you remove from a car, and still have a car?

You can take away the headlights, the hood ornament, and even the windows. You can take out the seats, as long as there's a place for the driver. You can strip off most of the body. It turns out, there is quite a lot you can remove from a car, and still have a car.

But once you get to the engine, and once you get to the

chassis, you really can't pull that off and still have what you can fairly call a car.[1]

For the last hundred years, people have been stripping away the essential truths of Christianity.

They started by stripping away the biblical account of creation, and they told us we were the product of chance—though we could still believe in God and Jesus, if we had to.

Soon, they began stripping away the historical validity of the Bible. Myth and propaganda, they said.

After that, they erased the miracles, because, of course, we live in a scientific age. Anti-supernaturalism is the new normal.

Then they said the Virgin Birth was a myth borrowed from pagan religion, but we could still believe in Jesus, because God was with him in a special way—just like he can be with us all.

Then they took away hell, because that's primitive, and besides, "love wins."

But they didn't stop there.

They essentially unbolted heaven, because, apparently it's all about the kingdom now. And good works now. And love now. A desire for a post-millennial, church-created, culture-healing Utopia on earth has all but eclipsed our longing for heaven.

They took away the sacredness of sex, and made it an animal impulse, or at least a social construct, and best not to judge anybody.

They dismantled the sacredness of life, and even made it a *sacrament* to kill the most vulnerable among us — young, old, and infirm.

Then they took away our Bibles—not technically, though. We still have our Bibles, but we don't use them, because we have a "fresh word of God by the Spirit," and we *feel* this is right, even though the Word of God says it is wrong. But feelings, emotions, subjective experiences, practicalities, and moments of "God showing up" have now been set above Scripture, so that even if we *say* we believe the Bible, we have no clue what's in it.

But they didn't stop. They began questioning everything. The deity of Christ. The humanity of Christ. Even the existence of Christ himself.

One day, they told us God is dead.

If God is dead, that meant they could take away the gospel. Because if there is no hell, who needs salvation?

Who needs an old Rugged Cross?

Who needs an urgent rescue from a danger that's been defined away as a relic of primitive religion?

Who needs an invitation to come to a Savior and have their sins be washed as white as snow?

If sins are just psychological problems that need comforting rather than a moral rebellion that necessitates divine retribution, why be saved?

Why be saved if joining the Church and fixing the world is all that matters? Who needs the gospel?

If the world could have its way, all we'd be left with is a minimalistic ethical system based on niceness, that is no different from any other religion or philosophy invented by the mind of mankind, except with a little Jesus sprinkled on top.

That stripped down version of Christianity is simply a car that won't go.

And it is miles away from the magnificent engine of truth that turned the world upside down.

It is instead a jangled heap of junkyard parts. It is a shell without a heart. It is epistemological chaos, and it just won't go.

BATTERING THE GATES OF HELL

Jesus said the Gates of Hell would not prevail against the Church. In that picture, the Church is on offense. In that picture, *we* are the ones battering down the gates of hell.

Why?

Because there are lost people in the devil's grip and they need to be saved.

xviii / AS GOES THE CHURCH

Inasmuch then as the children have partaken of flesh and blood, He Himself likewise shared in the same, that through death He might destroy him who had the power of death, that is, the devil, and release those who through fear of death were all their lifetime subject to bondage. (Hebrews 2:14, 15)

We're the ones who are supposed to be battering down the gates of hell.

We're on offense in the picture Jesus draws.

But that's not happening.

The reality is we're not on offense; we're on defense.

We can understand that the world would do this to us. Secular universities. So-called professors and experts spouting hatred of Christ with their unexamined presuppositions.

The world has never been a friend of Christianity. Paul said, "For Your sake we are killed all day long; / We are accounted as sheep for the slaughter" (Romans 8:36). The world is not a friend of the Church.

We can understand why. The gospel message is a huge insult to the secular mind. Who wants to be called a sinner? Who wants to be dethroned from the top of the heap? Who wants a God they must bow to? Who wants a Lord they must obey?

No, the world never has been, and never will be, a friend of the people of God. When the dismantling of our precious faith comes from the world, we can understand that.

But that's not our biggest problem.

Our biggest problem is that the dismantling of Christianity is happening from within.

It is Christians who are eating Christianity from the inside out.

- Biblical illiteracy is at an all time high.
- Local church evangelism is at an all time low.
- Sexual confusion and permissiveness is on the rise.

- Theological indifference and consequent ignorance rules the day.
- Shallow, superficial Christian messaging is everywhere you turn — in books, in worship music, in pulpits.
- We find story time in the pulpit, instead of fire-hoses of doctrine.
- We see untrained preachers spreading confusion over the gospel, and even more confusion over the Christian way of life.
- Only 6 percent of American churches are classified as "evangelistically effective." What does that say about the 94 percent? Pity the world's lost sheep.
- Worship experiences often prioritize subjective emotions above the Word of God.
- We discover the virtual inability of our pastors, much less our people, to couple, "It is written," with, "Thus saith the Lord," and then to take our stand there, on that sacred Scripture, come hell or high water.
- Too often we find the substitution of a social gospel that can only bandage a gaping wound, in the place of the supernatural gospel of saving grace, that alone can deliver from the one wound behind all the wounds of society — the wound called sin.

I can understand that the world would bend every effort to dismantle biblical Christianity... but the Church?

Why are we dismantling ourselves?

Why is the Church dismantling the car of "the faith once delivered to the saints?"

As goes the Church, so goes the world.

Chaos in the Church, means chaos in the world.

Warning after warning has gone unheeded.

Did we think God wasn't looking?

Did we think it was okay?

Did we imagine for a moment that we were actually entitled to his blessing?

Delusion.

Insanity.

THE CRISIS

I am writing this opening chapter in the midst of a global pandemic and economic crisis. The rest of this book had already been written over the course of two years.

It makes no difference. The sad fact is that every time we experience a national crisis, the Church returns to God in a very big way. It is beautiful to behold. But once the crisis begins to ease, we return to our stunted and chaotic sense of normal and nothing has changed.

God help us.

Whatever else you might say about this pandemic—whether you attribute it to God, or to the devil, or both—one thing we know for sure: *in the blink of an eye, the mightiest nation on earth has been brought to its knees.*

A booming economy.

An invincible military.

Everything's great!

Then in about a minute, we found ourselves shut down by microscopic invaders.

The Bible says, "Blessed is the nation whose God is the Lord" (Psalm 33:12).

But how can the Lord be the God of our nation, if he's barely the God of the Church?

As goes the Church, so goes the nation.

If he had found just ten righteous people, God would have spared Sodom (Genesis 18:32).

Though Jerusalem and Judah were devastated, had it not been for a "remnant" of faithful ones, they would have been utterly destroyed (Isaiah 1:9).

By the days of Jeremiah, God would have pardoned

Jerusalem could he find even one truth-seeker (Jeremiah 5:1).

The fortunes of the broader populace hinge on the faithfulness of the believing core.

King David laments the extinction of godliness and faithfulness among God's people. In times like this, "vileness is exalted" in the land, he said (Psalm 12:1,8). Even the land is subject to the condition of the Church.

As goes the Church, so goes the world.

> – THE FORTUNES OF THE BROADER POPULACE HINGE
> ON THE FAITHFULNESS OF THE BELIEVING CORE.

Yet there is hope. Whenever God's own people return to him in humility and truth, God stands ready to heal the land. We will show examples of this in later chapters.

> If My people who are called by My name will humble themselves, and pray and seek My face, and turn from their wicked ways, then I will hear from heaven, and will forgive their sin and heal their land. (2 Chronicles 7:14)

We, the Church, hold the keys to the kingdom. We, God's people, are the watchmen on the walls, the salt of the earth, the pillar and ground of the truth.

When the Church is sick, we are all sick. Chaos in the Church means chaos in the world.

THE WORLD IS NOT THE CHURCH

I never expect that the world should act like the Church. But I've got to expect that the Church should act like the Church.

An older and perhaps wiser generation of evangelical leaders often highlighted three priorities of the Church: *Exaltation*, *Edification*, and *Evangelism*.

Simply put, we are to exalt God in worship and praise, edify the saints principally through the Scriptures and prayer, and evangelize a lost and dying world by proclaiming the gospel and summoning all people to faith in Christ.

When the Church lets any other priorities rise to the fore-front, she cracks open a Pandora's box of competing priorities, and the result is chaos.

We're not here to legislate morality. We're not here to wrestle over the levers of political power. We're not here to preach just another system of morality.

We are here to storm the gates of hell, that we might rescue the perishing.

We are here to speak of a God in heaven, and of his Word on earth.

We are here to declare a comprehensive truth-claim so magnificent, and so coherent, and so life-giving that human minds could never have invented it.

We are here to do the most loving thing a human can do, which is to tell everybody who will listen of a Savior and of an Old Rugged Cross and of a home in heaven that alone gives meaning to our crazy pilgrimage on earth.

THE OTHER PLAGUE

In the early 1500s, the Bubonic Plague hit Europe. With a 70 percent mortality rate, and one day from onset to unconscious-ness, this little monster was spread by fleas.

Into that darkness, a young pastor and his wife ministered to the sick, always under the shadow of death. You might know them as Martin Luther and his wife Katie von Bora.

Yet, in the face of that plague—that spawn of Satan—God used Luther to recover two doctrines that are absolutely essen-tial for the Church to go forward. Doctrines that had been lost, buried in the chaos of a church that had lost its way.

Those two doctrines were:

- Number one: the authority of Scripture.

- Number two: the doctrine of justification by faith
  — the gospel of grace.

When the Church recovered those doctrines, there was such a revival in the Church that the unsaved world flooded into the family of faith in record numbers.

That's the hope, and that's where this book is headed. We will come back to these things.

For now, I am pleading with the Church to go back to the basics.

We cannot fix the world unless we restore the Church.

Oh let us rise up to be soldiers of the Cross, so that it can be truly said, Christ is building his Church, and the gates of hell are not prevailing against it.

A PRAYER

Gracious Lord,

We say with Job, "I have heard of You by the hearing of the ear, / But now my eye sees You. Therefore I abhor myself, / And repent in dust and ashes" (Job 42:5, 6).

We the church confess again our utter and abject need of you. We acknowledge your faithfulness and your grace, even as we confess our unworthiness apart from Christ.

We say, dear Lord, revive your church. We have a burden which we must lay before you, and ask your help in it. We mourn over the condition of your church. On every side, and even within, we see people endeavoring to undermine the doctrines of the everlasting Gospel.

Awaken us from our apathy. Stir us from our complacency.

We would ask you to revive a deep spirituality within the hearts of your own children. Make us holy by Christ within, our Great Sanctifier.

Lord, we do not love you as we should, because we do not know you deeply enough through the Sacred Scriptures. Many times we grow lukewarm. Doubt creeps over us, and unbelief mars our confidence. We sin, and we forget our God.

O Lord, help us!

How thankful we are for our never-ending pardon in Christ — yet at the same time, we pray that you would hasten our holiness, and strengthen your sanctifying work in us.

Open the heavens and come down, and pour out a fresh awareness of your majesty and grace upon your people through the study of your Word.

Lord, build your church, and grant that the gates of hell will not prevail.

Lord, restore the deep things of Scripture to the pulpits of our land.

Lord, restore our fortunes.

Bless us now, as we commit ourselves, and our nation, afresh to you, recognizing you have first committed yourself to us, even to the point of death.

Through Christ Our Lord,
Amen.

---

1. Credit for the car analogy goes to Michael Green in *The Truth of God Incarnate.*

PART 1
DISTURBING TRENDS IN TODAY'S CHURCH

1 / BRING BACK THE GIANTS

THERE WERE GIANTS in the land. Crowds gathered. Hearts opened. The greatest message ever conceived among humankind pushed back the darkness and fueled generations of heaven's ambassadors. Henrietta Mears, William R. Newell, Donald Grey Barnhouse, Harry Ironside, Ray Stedman, D. Martyn Lloyd-Jones, Arno C. Gabelein, E.K. Bailey, Warren Wiersbe, Romell Williams, W.A. Criswell. A legion more. Forgotten giants. They were nineteenth- and twentieth-century evangelical preachers and teachers of God's invincible Word. They opened the Scriptures and invited audiences to open their Bibles with them. They brought forth treasures. Their listeners' hearts burned within.

They were not known for charisma, humor, or eloquence. They did not promote themselves. They had no social media platforms. No gimmicks in their arsenal. Their clothing and style were conventional to a fault. Nothing hip. Nothing cool. They would describe themselves not as "visionary leaders," but as expositors of the sacred Scriptures.

Crowds did not follow them because they were glib story-tellers. Crowds followed them because they were fire hoses of doctrine, and the people were parched deserts, eager to be saturated with the living water of God.

They were Bible expositors first and foremost. They taught verse-by-verse, and sometimes word-by-word. They did not rush. They did not preach three messages in a row and call it "a series." They lingered over great texts. D. Martin Lloyd-Jones preached 366 sermons on the book of Romans and 255 on the Gospel of John. His sanctuaries were as packed as his sermons.

They weren't after a practical application that would last a few days and fizzle by Wednesday. They were simple without being simplistic. Nor did they manipulate emotion. They were after a slow, methodical transformation that would last a lifetime. They threw the Bible Bus into low gear, and churned up every inch of biblical pavement, slowly and methodically. Not hype. Not a pep rally. But the patient construction of a theological edifice in the soul—one that could withstand the storms of life, and uphold a beacon of the gospel in this tempestuous world.

They did not shy from the Scripture's great theological vocabulary. When they ran across the word *justification*, they paused their exegetical progress to explain it. Not in a glib, simplistic fashion, but in its wondrous depths. They shifted the exegetical transmission into neutral. They traced out the all-important distinction between being *declared* righteous (justification, a crisis at salvation) and being *made* righteous (sanctification, a process post-conversion), thus preserving the only foundation for salvation by grace through faith. Having explained the word, they then explained exactly how it fit in the particular context of Scripture they were teaching. Their privileged listeners felt the wonder of what God had done for them. When finished, they put their teaching back in gear, and moved on to the next verse or phrase.

Meat, not milk.

They unfolded the glorious doctrines of redemption, propitiation, regeneration, and expiation. They painted indelible pictures of a God who was sovereign, omnipotent, and omnipresent. They reveled in the sacred vocabulary of faith, thus equipping listeners to read their Bibles with understanding, while simultaneously rehabilitating countless souls drunk on the devil's lies.

They proclaimed Christ. They majored in the apostolic preaching of the Cross. They preached theology. They never shied away from deep truths, because they knew that it was only in the depths that their listeners would be "transformed by the renewing of their minds."

Though they had great persuasive powers, these giants always pointed away from themselves to the authority of Scripture. "Don't listen to me," they said, "listen to God's Word." They put their finger on a word in Scripture, and said, "Look at that. Do you see what this means?" The eyes of their listeners looked down into their Bibles to find the truth, rather than up and to the speaker's mouth. They were table-waiters, carrying a feast of God's Word to hungry souls. "Thus saith the Lord, hear ye him."

They gave more than three points on how to be a better husband, wife, boyfriend, or girlfriend. They ventured far beyond "practical" advice on finances or dating or personal success. They sent forth an army to change the world, but they equipped it first. They refused to deliver sermonettes, convinced these would only produce Christianettes. The invisible warfare demanded muscle, and they ran theological boot camps to build it.

When a church leader wondered aloud to the newly appointed pastor of London's famed Westminster Chapel, G. Campbell Morgan, whether the people of his church would "tolerate" expository preaching, Morgan said, "They're going to have to."

They were giants.

We, by comparison, are stunted.

STUNTED

Today, the center of gravity has shifted. The church is top-heavy. She has lost her ballast. Some of the biggest names in evangelical Christianity developed their followings while possessing little theological training or study. They unintentionally undermined the authority of Scripture – by omission at best, but occasionally by commission – as they pointed more to the so-called "fresh" word than to the settled words of Scripture.

And so we crack open the door to chaos.

To their credit, some of these leaders have taken time to backfill their theological training. May God increase their tribe.

"Chapter and verse," our grandparents' generation demanded.

"Tell us a story," today's postmodern generation cries. They forget that every time Jesus told a story, he left listeners confused to the point of exasperation. And never mind that he explicitly crafted his parables to *conceal* truth from outsiders (Luke 8:10, Mark 4:11,12).

Suckled on tolerance, addicted to sweetener, committed to a good time had by all, suffocated by unrelenting calls to activism, today's evangelicalism wades in the shallow end of the biblical pool, even as western civilization dies of theological thirst.

The main seminary degree for pastoral training is called the Master of Divinity (M.Div.). It is a jack-of-all trades professional degree, to prepare pastors for local church work. A little bit of leadership, counseling, church history, and a whole lot of Bible and theology. A generation ago, the M.Div. almost uniformly required studies in both Hebrew and Greek. Today, most seminaries only require one or the other, not both – if they require either at all.

We would not go to a doctor who could not speak the language of human anatomy – how much less should we entrust our souls to pastors who cannot speak, or at least access through sheer tenacity, the language of divine things in Scripture.

Yesterday's seminaries required numerous courses in the

numerous subjects of theology: Theology proper (the attributes and nature of God), Bibliology, Christology, Soteriology (the doctrine of salvation), Hamartiology (the doctrine of sin and the Fall), Anthropology (biblical teaching on human nature, origins, and destiny), Pneumatology (the doctrine of the Holy Spirit), Ecclesiology (the doctrine of the church), Angelology (includes Satanology), and Eschatology (the doctrine of last things).

By the time I was in seminary, those many courses were clustered into three courses.

Today, many schools batch them into just one or two courses in Christian theology.

Imagine lawyers going into practice with only one or two classes in law.

Seminary preparation has in too many cases become more about the *process* of theologizing – endless circling with questions – than about the *content* of theology – actually landing on theological terrain, staking out a position and supporting it scripturally, all the while understanding and remaining charitable toward those with whom we disagree.

There is a festering theological illiteracy in the land, and by land, I mean the leadership in the church today.

We are top-heavy. We have lost our ballast, our *gravitas*, and are in danger of being toppled in the next big storm.

I am not saying that a seminary degree is required to either pastor flocks or to be used mightily of God. Charles Spurgeon was self-taught. He possessed a voracious appetite for theology and doctrine, and he changed his world, and still influences it from the grave.

He studied himself full of *gravitas*. His library stands as a testament to both his theological appetite and his genius.

Too many of today's leaders do no study at all.

They have good hair and great fashion.

They "borrow" pre-made sermon series, graphics included, from the celebrity preacher *du jour*.

They can preach sexy sermons that suck in crowds. They

can wave their wands to produce an emotional high with a glory-cloud-chaser, topped with a Bible-verse cherry.

They are charismatic personalities, inconsistent in their theology, preaching moralistic messages, emotional hype, and sentimental love notes to Jesus. They live on the mundane plain, never scaling the transcendent heights of Scripture, because they don't even know the heights are there to scale.

Lightweights.

"Visionary" leaders.

Leaders more than teachers.

Inspirers more than instructors.

When was the last time God's people flocked to a Bible Conference?

Where are the great teachers of the Bible? Where are those who bring the deep things of God to life? Who is preaching the great apostolic doctrines that turned the world upside down?

And where are those who couple such truths with evangelistic appeals where people actually – gasp – get saved?

God is weeping for his flock and is not happy with his shepherds.

When I first entered pulpit ministry, I was taught to focus on nothing but preaching and evangelism for my first year.

My preaching professors urged us to devote an hour in the study for every minute in the pulpit. Preaching a forty-minute message? Better spend forty hours in the Word.

Unthinkable.

Laughable.

Antiquated.

We have too much "loving-on" people to do, and too much "leadership" to demonstrate to waste our time in the most loving form of leadership there is: prepping in the secret chambers to feed starving souls the life-giving Word.

We are in a perilous state, in this condition of stunted growth. Immaturity reigns. Chaos follows.

Today, it's about "leadership," numerical growth, crafting "experiences," superficial behavior-change, spending time with people, listening, loving on people, being accessible, Holy Spirit, Holy Spirit, Holy Spirit, cheerleading, organizing, strategizing, giving back, being practical, and bringing entrepreneurial skills to the leadership of the church. Where's the meat?

We evangelicals call ourselves heirs of the apostles. Let us heed, then, the apostolic marching orders:

> It is not desirable that we should leave the word of God and serve tables... But we will give ourselves continually to prayer, and to the ministry of the word. (Acts 6:2,4)

Christ *should* spew us out of his mouth.

Not because these endless rounds of pastoral activism are bad, but because they create addictive delivery systems for impotent content.

Back to the Bible! Back to the Bible in its richness and depth!

There are exceptions to this chaos, and no doubt you've been thinking of some as you read. Thank God.

But they are exceptions, and that's the problem.

Dorothy Sayers saw it coming, way back in the World War II era.

> The one thing I am here to say to you is this: that it is worse than useless for Christians to talk about the importance of Christian morality, unless they are prepared to take their stand upon the fundamentals of Christian theology. It is a lie to say that dogma [doctrine] does not matter; it matters enormously. It is fatal to let people suppose that Christianity is only a mode of feeling; it is virtually necessary to insist that it is first and foremost a rational explanation of the universe. It is hopeless to offer Christianity as a vaguely idealistic aspiration of a simple and consoling kind; it is, on the contrary, a hard, tough, exacting, and complex doctrine, steeped in a drastic and uncompromising realism. And it is

fatal to imagine that everybody knows quite well what Christianity is and needs only a little encouragement to practice it. The brutal fact is that in this Christian country not one person in a hundred has the faintest notion about what the church teaches about God or man or society or the person of Jesus Christ. [Dorothy Sayers in Creed and Chaos]

"A hard, tough, exacting, and complex doctrine, steeped in a drastic and uncompromising realism." Hardly the language of today's popular pastors.

Oh, they are hard, tough, and exacting in their legalistic imperatives – sacrifice, give, serve, go, do, commit – to be sure – but not in the rigor of their theological instruction. In matters of theology, it's tepid cream of rice every single week.

Even worse, since those legalistic imperatives remain utterly divorced from the theological truth-system that, a) explains why they are important, and b) empowers them with supernatural strength, they only produce dead works of the flesh, which remain perpetually displeasing to God.

The people of God do not grow by being hen-pecked with how to behave.

The people of God grow by being fed the blood-red meat of God's inerrant Word.

God, save our pulpits.

Save the church from itself.

Please, Lord, give us giants once again.

REVERSING THE TREND

"Expository preaching should provide the main diet of preaching for a Christian community. . . . [It] is the best method for displaying and conveying your conviction that the whole Bible is true. This approach testifies that you believe every part of the Bible to be God's Word, not just particular themes and not just the parts you feel comfortable agreeing with." (Tim Keller, *Preaching*, 32)

As newborns cry for their milk, so let the people of God clamor for their biblical exposition. It is time to regain our muscle by feeding God's people the whole counsel of God. This can only happen when we let the Bible not only answer questions, but tell us what questions to ask, by preaching through whole books.

Otherwise, we are left with the "Meme-ification" of the Scriptures, as teachers turn the sacred text into sharable slogans divorced from their theological, historical, and canonical contexts, and therefore separated from their life-transforming power.

I do not claim that restoring expository preaching will fix everything that's wrong in evangelicalism. But it is a non-negotiable start. It lays down rails for everything else. If we say we are Bible-believing at the core, then let's prove it. Let the Bible speak for itself, and let the Bible set the agenda for what it speaks on.

Nor would I lay down any legalistic imperative that all preaching series must be expository. As Keller says, it's to be "the main diet," not the only diet. My personal practice has been to alternate New Testament books, with Old Testament books, and with Topical Series—ideally timing the topical series for the more sporadic summer crowd. Even so, with tongue in cheek, Walter Kaiser has suggested "preachers should preach a topical sermon only once in five years—and then immediately repent and ask God's forgiveness!"[1]

Chuck Smith ignited a kind of west coast revival when he preached verse-by-verse through Romans at the original Calvary Chapel. D. Martyn Lloyd-Jones transformed a blue-collar coal-mining community by preaching theologically meaty expository series through whole books of the Bible in

Wales. Luther and Calvin produced verse by verse commentaries on the whole Bible, largely the product of their preaching labors. They changed the face, not only of Christianity, but of the world.

The Bible is powerful.

We should try using it.

Dear pastor, preacher, Sunday School teacher, small group leader, or seminary professor—open your Bible to Ephesians or Ruth or John or Ezra, and lead your group through it verse by verse. If you don't have time to preach through larger books, preach through units, such as Romans 9-11 or the Joseph narrative in Genesis 37-50. You will be shocked how the Holy Spirit coordinates the timing of each message with the deepest needs of your people.

Perhaps the mother of all maladies of our theologically chaotic church is her nutritional deficiency. The sugar-rush of inspirational, topical, behavioral preaching may draw a crowd, but it will never mature that crowd. For that, we need solid meat.

Lord, raise up an army of expositors, giants in the land who will feed your sheep.

---

1. Walter Kaiser. *Toward an Exegetical Theology* (Grand Rapids: Baker Academic, 1998) p. 19.

IF YOU WISH to rant about the state of affairs in the contemporary church, worship music is low-hanging fruit, I know. God
help us.

The burden of this book is that God's people have
welcomed chaos into the church and our lives. Sometimes, our
worship music is both a symptom and a contributing factor.

And let me say right away it's not just the repetition that's
to blame.

In the worship song commonly called "Psalm 136," you
will find the words "his mercy endures forever" 26 times in 26
verses. I'd call that repetitious. Repetition *per se* is not the
problem.

Arguably the greatest extra-biblical worship song of all time
– one that the church has stood up for ever since King George
II launched the tradition at its 1742 debut – is Handel's
Hallelujah Chorus. This chorus repeats the word Hallelujah at
least 36 times, King of kings 8 times, Lord of lords 8 times, and
for ever and ever 12 times. And I'm not even counting the
echoes. The finale is nothing but repetition:

> *King of kings*
> *And Lord of lords*

> *King of kings*
> *And Lord of lords*
> *And He shall reign for ever and ever*
> *King of kings*
> *And Lord of lords*
> *Hallelujah! Hallelujah!*
> *Hallelujah! Hallelujah!*

Repetition is not the core problem in contemporary worship music.

The core problem is that worship music is written all too often by worship leaders who can strum a guitar and sing decently and have never swum to the deep end of theology's pool.

They don't even know it's there.

The deepest thing they can say about God is, "He's a good, good, good, good God," like a good, good dog, so we can demand he fetch us a blessing.

Yes, God is good. In theology, this is called the Benevolence of God, and is a doctrine rich in meaning. Yet I suspect not one worship leader in a hundred has bothered to crack open the theology books and launch a voyage into the wonders of this theology before they pen their ditties. They cannot deliver the depths of divine benevolence because they haven't even heard the word, much less studied it out.

We get the impression that the primary method of writing a contemporary worship hit is to first run the lyrics through the Random Phrase Generator, to produce a collection of Twitter-sized fragments assembled into a series of non-sequiturs, colored by mixed-metaphors to be sung at gradually swelling volume with maximum *pathos*. Little concern *logos*, or for cadence, and even less for the poetry's beauty.

So the church hums along in the theological shallows. There is little content to make our hearts skip a beat. All too many songwriters are incapable of painting a picture of a God so grand he takes our breath away, because they have rarely gone there themselves. So the church stands and watches while song leaders do their thing and the people on stage have their own little worship moment, eyes closed, bodies swaying, congregation forgotten.

The hymns I learned as a boy in church, I still sing today when I walk my dog in the early morning hours. I doubt that anybody will be singing many of today's praise songs thirty years from now as they walk along. There's no "there" there.

As all the church grandparents are nodding their heads in self-righteous disapproval, let me say that the fat, old hymnal has had the benefit of centuries of culling. There were plenty of horrible hymns composed back in the day. The large majority of them, no doubt. They just didn't stand the test of time, so the church spit them out. Don't be so smug, fellow Curmudgeons.

And please don't complain it's too loud. If you don't like the music, any volume is too loud. I've been to churches where the pipe organ rumbles your chest at about 110 decibels, and all the old folks love it because it's *Holy, Holy, Holy.* Every generation needs to be evangelized on their own terms. So volume is relevant. Let's just not compromise on biblically meaningful lyrics. Everything else is up for grabs.

Today's worship music has a shelf-life of about six weeks.

Praise God from whom all blessings flow.

We've chewed all the flavor out of its gum by then.

Compounding this problem is a generation of worshipers suckled on a one-dimensional God of love. Songs about holiness? Spiritual warfare? The Second Coming? Divine Wrath? Omnipotence? The Incarnation and what it means? The Cross? Justification? Redemption? Propitiation (God forbid!)? The Holy Spirit? The Power of Scripture? The Resurrection? Calvary? Prayer?

A contemporary worship song on these theological topics is almost impossible to find.

Instead we have an endless succession of songs so saccharin that any church singing them on the way to battle Satan would doom itself to crushing defeat. Indeed, they'd turn tail and run before the battle could be joined, right after sticking a daisy in Satan's muzzle.

Worship music has become a generic zombie, a husk of its former self, lurching across the land, infiltrating every church that's even halfway contemporary.

Sound and fury, signifying nothing. Saying nothing important beautifully.

I am not arguing for a return to the hymnal. That is not the heart-music of today's generation. It will drive younger generations away. I love the old hymnal because it's deep *and I grew up with it.* But for the majority who did not grow up with it, the hymnal is not the solution. I am not arguing for that.

I am arguing for theological depth and breadth (both) among songwriters. I am arguing for correct doctrine and more of it in our songs. I am pleading for songwriters to write thematically on the whole range of systematic theology. I am asking that you pick a theme-say the faithfulness of God—and then actually *develop* it. Focus on it throughout the whole song, and plumb the theological depths of this one singular theme throughout the entire song. For example:

> *Great is Thy faithfulness, O God my Father*
> *(theme stated)!*
> *There is no shadow of turning with Thee (theme*
> *restated poetically by citing James 1:17).*
> *Thou changest not (correctly rooting divine*
> *faithfulness within immutability, citing*
> *Malachi 3:6),*
> *Thy compassions, they fail not (application of*
> *immutability/faithfulness, citing*
> *Lamentations 3:22),*
> *As Thou hast been, Thou forever wilt be (can I*
> *get an amen?!).*

The composer is drilling down into a divine attribute, with

focus, theological awareness, scriptural integrity, and beautiful poetry.

A little more of that please.

PREOCCUPATION WITH ITSELF

Perhaps the deepest, most subtle problem in current Christian worship music is its preoccupation with itself. By this, I mean worship music about worship music.

When I look through a window, I hope to see the snow-capped mountains and forested valleys outside. I want to be caught up in their splendor and taken aback by their beauties. I do not look to see the window, I look to see through it to what lies beyond. If there is, however, a smudge on the window, then the wonders of what's out there get obscured, and my attention is diverted to the window.

Worship music is a window through which I hope to see the wonders of God. Give me a glimpse of his attributes, nature, names, and works. I long to sing the mighty power of God, to revel in his immutability, and to linger over his illimitable sovereignty and grace. Therein lies my hope.

But there is too much of the first person in our lyrics. The whole song is a smudge on the glass. It's about itself. It's about the act of worship rather than the God whom we worship. The I and the We obscure the He.

When I sing, "I worship You," I have said nothing about God and everything about what I'm doing. I am stuck, like a smeared bug carcass, on the glass. When I sing a song about praises, I have not praised God, I have praised praise. When the worship leader cajoles me to worship better, I am stuck on the glass of worship, and have been given no sense of the grandeur of the God whom I worship.

If I sing about my hands upraised, my heart tuned to praise, my face turned down to the ground, and my heart split open by love, I have sung praises to my praises and sung nothing about God.

A classic saying applies here: "For every look at self, take ten looks at Christ."

"One look at his dear face" brings peace to the chaos of our lives. Please, dear worship leader and songwriter, lead us away from ourselves that we may "turn our eyes upon Jesus."

THE WORSHIP WAR IRONY

We cannot leave a topic as ripe for critique as music without noting what just might be the greatest irony of our times.

Back in the misty days before Worship War I, church music sounded like church music. An organ. A piano. A choir. A soloist. A quartet. Or some permutation of these. Everybody knows what church music sounded like, because the only places you heard it were a) church, and b) funerals. It was instantly recognizable as church music. When we tuned across the radio dial, we knew right away when we were hearing [evil] rock, [tolerable] country, talk radio, or church music. It took a nano-second, because of its unmistakable sound.

For those of us who grew up with church music, it holds a warm place in our hearts. It is the music of our lives, and it is, to us, sacred.

For those who did not grow up in the church, church music sounded alien and off-putting.

So, along came Larry Norman to scream the question, "Why should the devil have all the good music?"

Great question.

This led to Worship War I. It birthed Christian rock bands like Rez, Petra, Servant, DeGarmo and Key, and Stryper.

Amy Grant's music was banned from the Christian bookstore at Moody Bible Institute. Such a radical!

Whatever else you might say about these upstart Christian artists, you cannot say they sounded like church music.

They sounded like the world's music. That is what made them so evil in the eyes of shocked church people.

They put sacred lyrics to a recognizable secular sound.

Anyone tuning across the dial for some good old fashioned rock and roll, might pause to listen. The songs no longer sounded like church music.

I am saying that the revolution in Christian music that happened back in the Worship War era was a fight to make church music sound like the world's music.

It was quite a fight. Only us gray-hairs remember it. We took sides. We split churches. We tried to blend it in with hymns, which only ticked off everybody. As a youth pastor I had a senior pastor order me to use nothing "more rocky" than Sandi Patty's *Via Dolarosa* (YouTube it).

My church had to endure a special speaker who came to talk about the evils of "so-called" Christian rock.

And must I remind you of backward masking?

Remember that? For any youngster reading this, backward masking was the accusation that if you spun your turntable backwards, many Christian rock artists had snuck satanic messages into their album's grooves to mess with your mind subliminally.

"The devil is your god." At least that's how they deciphered the gibberish you heard spinning an album backwards.

The world had gotten into the church, and Satan was dancing with delight.

All because church music suddenly began to sound like the world's music.

HILLSONGIZATION

Disclaimer: I did not invent the term I am about to share — sociologists did.

It is the term *Hillsongization.* It is a recognition of the enormous influence Hillsong Church, and publishing partners such as Jesus Culture (a subsidiary of Bethel Church, in my home town), have exerted on the sound of today's church music.

I like much of this sound. It is the new music of my heart, to a degree. But I'm a church person, don't forget.

And recently, I woke up from a dream.

As a guy who advocated for yesterday's worship wars, I now scratch my head. What happened?

Our church music is now largely homogenized. You can pick it out. Whether you tune across YouTube channels, or Spotify options, you can pick out church music right away. It has a distinct sound all its own, and it's everywhere.

Have you visited churches or campuses from place to place? I just attended a chapel service at a west coast Christian college, and I could swear I heard all the same music done in exactly the same way as the conference I was just at three hundred miles away.

Congratulations, Church.

We're back where we started.

Church music sounds like church music.

Again.

It is instantly recognizable as church music. It doesn't sound like anything else. It isn't quite rock and roll. It isn't quite country. It isn't quite pop. It's neither EDM, R&B, jazz, or hip hop. It's church music.

Welcome to Ground Hog Day. Back in the Worship War I days, we wanted desperately to make music the world could relate to, *for the sake of evangelism,* especially among the unchurched.

Today, we've turned inward again.

Will somebody please wrap some meaningful sacred lyrics into worldly musical garb — pick a style, any style — and let's sing *that* in church.

I hereby declare war.

Let Worship War 2.0 commence!

REVERSING THE TREND

Please, worship leader and songwriter, please say something so wondrous about God that the worship just gushes out of me. Find the transcendence. I'm begging you. Say it. Quote it from Scripture. Cite it from a theology book. Quote a pithy line from Spurgeon. Tell me a wonder, any wonder, about who God is and what he has done, and I will praise my Wondrous Redeemer.

Your job, like that of the Psalmist, is to craft words — hammering them like gold and pounding them into shape — until they sparkle with the transcendence of God. As any author will tell you, pounding words into shape is hard work. It is not for the shallow or faint of heart.

It requires great depth and maturity in the Lord. So, we're counting on you.

I can't blame just the songwriters, though. I have to blame us pastors for giving you such devitalized raw material.

If you want me to worship, don't tell me to worship. And don't rely on the instrumentation to make me worship. Your crescendo on the tenth repetition doesn't make it any deeper than the first. It's not about that.

It is, instead, about painting on my imagination a portrait of God so scary-beautiful he makes me want to stand and salute before you even tell me to.

Worship music exists to reinforce doctrine. It serves to drive doctrine past our academic mentality into our passion-driven spirit. Doctrine exists to acquaint us with God in ways so biblically profound he astonishes us.

The scriptural knowledge of God elicits worship.

Everything else, therefore, should serve up this scriptural knowledge in poetic form.

If the subject of worship is God, and if we are going to have worship pastors, it follows that they must master not only music, but the doctrine of God.

This topic is called Theology Proper, and worship pastors

must soak in it. They must dig into the meat of Scriptures. They should be able to rattle off fifty names of God and a dozen divine attributes. They must know the outline of Trinitarian theology, and be conversant with Christ's hypostatic union. They must know the salvation doctrines of justification, redemption, and propitiation. And they must know both Scriptures and beautiful ways to state these doctrines. In fact, they should drink from the well of all the topics of systematic theology, including good old premillennial songs about Jesus coming again.

Worship leaders are, after all, part of the window. They should become invisible. They must master the art of pointing beyond themselves to the majesties of God and his salvation in the language of both Scripture and of the people. That will elicit a kind of worship all the scolding — and all the tattoos, piercings, and skinny jeans in the world — won't do.

If worship leaders flourish in the knowledge of God, we all flourish. If they sip meekly at theology, they only nurture the chaos.

Come on Worship Leader! Belly up to the bar of Theology Proper and drink deeply. Our spiritual lives depend on it.

Let God be all in all.

Most of all, in our worship music.

SOME THINGS ARE TRUE. Some things are false. You might get an argument about that.

Some people go to heaven. Some people go to hell. Jesus is the only way to heaven. You will definitely get an argument about that, tragically, even from those who call themselves evangelicals.

The Church can either warn people to flee from the wrath to come, or, in the name of so-called tolerance, spit on substitutionary atonement and define into meaninglessness the Cross of Christ. There is no middle ground.

Such "Particularism," as it is called, though eminently biblical, is enormously unpopular in our age of secular intolerance. It also turns out to be unpopular to many good, church-going people too.

Whatever became of hell? The simple fact of it will never change. To extinguish the fires of hell is to diminish grace and to disrespect the Cross. It is to put the world we serve into grave peril. If we Christians offer a Savior, what, exactly, is he saving us from?

Generations of Christians have staunchly maintained a binary vision of the eternal state: the redeemed enjoy the bliss of heaven and the unredeemed suffer the fires of hell. This doctrine dates back to the foundations of the Christian faith and beyond. Michael Green, in his classic study on evangelism in the early church, wrote:

> A clear dualism runs through every strand of the gospel record of Jesus's teaching. Mankind is divided into those who accept Him as the way to God and those who do not. There are two ways a man may tread—the broad way which leads to destruction or the narrow way which leads to life: no third option. Entry into the kingdom of God depends upon a relationship with Jesus. Always we meet this religious dualism. It is one of the most objectionable elements in the gospel to modern man. No doubt it was to men of the first century, but those Christians believed implicitly that Jesus was the only hope for the world, and the only way to God for the human race.[1]

The fires of hell have always stoked the engine of world mission and evangelism. Green noted:

> Now if you believe that outside of Christ there is no hope, it is impossible to possess an atom of human love and kindness without being gripped with a great desire to bring men to this one way of salvation.[2]

MORE THAN PAPER

The doctrine of eternal damnation is painful and complex, and there are a number of positions one might take while remaining within the realm of orthodoxy. Yet the doctrine has always been seen as *essential*. Virtually all evangelical institutions affirm two destinies, one of salvation in Christ alone, and the other of a Christless eternity under the condemnation of God — with the determination made prior to death based upon faith or unbelief in Christ.

But that's on paper.

Today's evangelical church has gone virtually silent on a bucketful of crucial doctrines. The Trinity. Heaven. Hell. The doctrines of the Cross. True grace. The doctrine of Union with Christ. The priority of evangelism. The authority and sufficiency of Scripture.

Our theological underpinnings are rotting away.

To erase hell is to redefine the Cross. No longer does Calvary offer the enormously costly sacrifice which alone can rescue us from a rightly earned divine wrath, it now only does something something about something something and, anyway, love.

To erase hell is to demote the Lord Jesus Christ. No longer does he stand as the human and divine Conqueror of Sin and the Shatterer of the Gates of Hell and the Absolute Monarch of our destinies, and the non-negotiable Lynchpin of Salvation. No. He is now a great guy who taught great stuff, and, um, well, grace.

Rob Bell's controversial 2011 book, *Love Wins,* put the final nail in hell's coffin. It's okay to kind of not believe in hell and there's this awesomely deep mystery, and let's just leave it up for grabs because I'm not God and who's to say, but as long as love wins, we can all not worry about it. Besides, talking about hell hurts people's feelings, and we turn people off that way.

Yes, Rob, truth does that. It turns people off. It is the sword that divides that Jesus actually talked about (Matthew 10:34).

But I can't blame Rob Bell. He only epitomized the pathetically bland teaching that had been creeping into evangelical churches for a long time.

I have to ask, who let these people through the doors? Who is publishing their error and why? Why is this even a discussion?

The same drive toward niceness and urge for relevancy that has driven theology out of our pulpits has driven hell out of our conversations.

So, let's not warn anybody to flee from the wrath to come; let's just invite them on a journey. And "love on" them.

The human heart was created for truth. When we understand God's truth and structure it into the deep places of our souls, we become increasingly aligned with reality as created by God. By this alignment, our souls create the internal structures of harmony and peace we all naturally crave.

But when we defy truth or deny it, we introduce fractures into our own psychology we were never meant to bear. Wherever chaos is found, it is a sign that truth is being neglected, ignored, or denied.

I am arguing that theological chaos in the Church is the root of the social, political, and emotional chaos we see playing out all around us.

Heaven and Hell turn out to be organizing principles for all of life. We erase them at our peril.

A NEW CREED

A study of religious youth in the early 2000s summarized the default spiritual position of the typical teenager under the new title of "Moralistic Therapeutic Deism."[3]

Researchers identified five basic tenets of this creed:

1. A god exists who created and ordered the world and watches over human life on earth.
2. God wants people to be good, nice, and fair to each other, as taught in the Bible and by most world religions.
3. The central goal of life is to be happy and to feel good about oneself.
4. God does not need to be particularly involved in one's life except when God is needed to resolve a problem.
5. Good people go to heaven when they die.[4]

When I read this list to my wife, a professor at a Christian university, she said, "That describes basically every one of my students."

A *Christian* university.

The precisely worded doctrinal statements and creeds, hammered out through centuries of discourse and intense study into the language and grammar of Scripture, have evaporated. In their place, we are offered insipid generalities from a band of Neo-Ninevites, too ignorant to know their spiritual right hand from their left.

Emergency!

Sound the alarm!

This Moralistic Therapeutic Deism is a threat to the church today. It is the greatest competitor to biblical Christianity because it crouches silently, like a virus, side-by-side with truly fervent Christians in the pews. It is making the church a pathetic shadow of its former self.

And so theological chaos eclipses centuries of bright clarity.

Let us parse the brilliant name given this new spiritual ideology.

- *Moralistic*: reducing the glorious edifice of Christian theology to a set of bland moral values based more on current consensus than on Scripture.
- *Therapeutic*: turning religion into a self-help, feel-good, primarily emotional stream of experience.
- *Deism*: God is out there, but only swoops in during emergencies, and is essentially an undemanding deity.

I ache with compassion for the upcoming generations. We have not served them well — not socially, not societally, not maritally, not theologically, and not ecclesiastically. We have buried the gold of a full-orbed theology beneath heaps of reputedly "relevant, caring, and practical" manure.

With that, we have buried hell.

We have quenched the fires of the fear of the Lord. We have doused any urgency over evangelism. We have abandoned our posts as watchmen and women on the walls (Ezekiel 33:6,7). We have turned Pascal's Wager on its head. By betting against hell, we have blood on our hands. On top of all that, we have smothered the only force that makes *grace* really and truly amazing.

There is no joy for me in this doctrine. R.W. Dale said only D.L. Moody had the right to preach about hell, because he always did it with a tear in his eye. May it be the same for me, and for all of us.

One day, long ago, God saved a little Italian boy from eternal damnation in the Lake of Fire — a fate I deserved.

I am forever grateful. And as often as I think of the cost, I am amazed. Thank you Jesus.

Too bad a growing body within the evangelical church recoils at the thought of saying the same.

---

1. Michael Green, *Evangelism in the Early Church* (Grand Rapids, MI: William B. Eerdmans Publishing Co., 1970), p. 249.
2. Ibid.
3. Christian Smith and Melina Lundquist Denton. *Soul Searching: The Religious and Spiritual Lives of American Teenagers*, Oxford University Press, 2009.
4. R. Albert Mohler, Jr., "Moralistic Therapeutic Deism—the New American Religion" in *The Christian Post*. April 18, 2005. Online at https://www.christianpost.com/news/moralistic-therapeutic-deism-the-new-american-religion.html. Retrieved, April 16, 2019.

I HAVE IN MY LIBRARY a worn out, orange, paperback book entitled *Basic Christian Doctrines,* first published in 1962 and then reprinted in 1971.[1]

I do not remember when I first picked up this book, but I do know I was in my twenties. I also recall wanting to be personally equipped to teach and defend these doctrines to the Awana leaders I served with.[2]

The book contains 45 chapters on the essential foundations of evangelical faith. Each chapter is written by a theological heavyweight of a bygone era. The whole work is edited by the late, great Carl F. H. Henry. Forty-five chapters, each one plumbing the depths, the nuances, and the distinctive features of evangelicalism's cardinal doctrines.

The book is remarkable to me today for two main reasons.

First, it uses the word *basic* in its title.

By today's standards, however, this book is anything but basic. It explores theology in deep and meaningful ways. It deals with nuances that would be lost on most modern Christians.

What I am saying is that what a past generation considered *basic,* today's generation would consider too advanced to bother with.

The book differentiates the communicable from the incommunicable attributes of God. It discusses Original Sin and the imputation of Adam's guilt. It opens up the doctrine of the Mystical Union between Christ and His people, and includes a chapter on the Kenotic Theory relative to the person of Christ.

If these are yesterday's *basics*, doesn't that indicate there is something radically different today?

A second equally disturbing reason I find the book remarkable is that each of its chapters was first published, not in some abstract theological journal, but in the popular level magazine *Christianity Today*. The theologically rich content of this book was considered suitable for the average Christian reader of its day.

In my estimation, the *seminary student* of today would have a hard time plowing through this book. Many pastors would struggle with it. Yet *Christianity Today* found it needful and suitable for its broad readership back in the day.

Something has changed.

I suspect that what has changed is the answer to a singularly important question which we must never stop asking.

That question is: *Where do you get your truth?*

The technical name for this topic is epistemology. Ever since Satan suckered Eve into questioning God's Word in the Garden of Eden, God's people have waged war against the downward pull of cheap epistemology.

CHEAP EPISTEMOLOGY

There is a growing roster of cheap substitutes for the in-depth teaching of the Word of God. These substitutes are cheap because they are imitations of the real thing. They are cheap because they are intellectually effortless. They are cheap because they capitulate to the spirit of the age, wimping out rather than confronting the destructive lies of our demonically hypnotized culture.

Dear Christian, where do you find your truth?

1. Contemporary opinion

A 2019 article in *Christian Headlines* described a seminary president who rejects the literal bodily resurrection of Christ. She also rejects the virgin birth, prayer for healing, and miracles. She has no faith in heaven, or life after death, yet she is the president of Union Theological Seminary. [3]

Of course this is the sad trend in liberal branches of theology. Once they discard the Bible, anything goes, including the teaching of Wicca and other forms of paganism in schools that were once solely devoted to the Word of God.

Apparently, they know better than the apostles and the prophets. They have the enlightened view of truth.

Yet they have dismantled so much of Christianity's car that it is an unrecognizable assemblage of parts.

Why would anyone accept the mantle of Christian leadership, and then dismantle the entire structure of biblical faith?

The only answer can be that they have exalted human reason and contemporary opinion above the authority of Scripture, doing what is right in their own eyes. This is the essence of cheap epistemology.

It is also narcissism on parade.

2. Experience

What do you call that gathering of God's people at 10:30 of your church? A mass? A worship service? An assembly?"

I don't care to quibble about the label. I just want to think about the recent trend of calling it an "experience." "Join us at the 10:30 experience."

Is that what we're crafting? Experiences? And what if attendees fail to *experience* something of note? Was the whole thing a flop? Such naming belies a faulty conception of the gathering of God's people.

At the heart of that conception squats the erroneous

assumption that if I don't *experience* it, nothing important happened.

It's worth considering this critique by the venerable D. Martyn Lloyd-Jones:

> I trust that you will also agree that deliberate attempts at 'conditioning' the people are surely thoroughly bad... for the moment I content myself with saying that this attempt to 'condition' the people, to soften them up, as it were, actually militates against the true preaching of the Gospel.[4]

Karl Barth maintained that the Word of God only "becomes" the Word of God when the reader "encounters" God in its pages. This neo-orthodoxy, as it came to be called, has insinuated itself into the current church culture. We're a church on an endless quest for experiences, encounters, and emotionally charged highs.

I would classify the desperate seeking for "signs and wonders" and other "manifestations of the Spirit" under this category. I will discuss this in a later chapter.

By this approach, church-goers are conditioned to require the experiential touch. They crave it. They can't wait for the next one. They demand it. They berate themselves if they don't get it. Worship leaders strain themselves to conjure an experience through an alchemy of repetitive chants, summonings of the Holy Spirit, digital pyrotechnics, and congregational scoldings.

The church remains intellectually empty even as they are over-stimulated experientially.

Experience *per se* qualifies as cheap epistemology because any secular speaker can put on a show with some razzle dazzle without one molecule of devotion to Christ or his gospel. The experiential trap is just another mode of entertainment, heat without light.

3. Emotion

Emotion and experience go hand in hand in that both are empirical modes of epistemology. There is something sensible and tangible in the moment that is said to be speaking God's truth to me.

Clichés such as, "Wow, God really showed up today" manifest this cheap epistemology.

Please don't get me wrong, I am all for emotion and experience in worship. Don't think for a moment that I am advocating a dry and sterile intellectualism in our churches. I am not. I believe in passion. I am a fan of laughter and weeping. I've been known to clap my hands and shout Amen. I am all for the full range of human emotion in our interactions with God... whenever the emotions are aligned with and prompted by biblical truth.

The simple fact is however that no emotion is revelatory. Reality doesn't care how you feel.

God has spoken decisively in His Word. Everything else is to be a response to that unchanging truth.

I have known people who have made painfully bad marriage choices, because *they felt* that God was speaking to them. I know people who have lifelong regrets from following an *emotion* that they attributed to the Spirit of God. I know people who entered ministry because they "felt something" only to wash out a short time afterwards, because the feeling went away.

When it comes to truth, emotion is a fickle and unreliable guide.

Again, I am not opposed to feelings. I am a big fan of following your heart. However, we must first follow the truth as God has revealed it in Scripture, and as it has been apprehended by our minds, long before we ever let our emotions take the helm.

Subjectivity and emotions turn out to be cheap epistemology and subtle ways of making a god out of self.

4. New Revelation, Inner Voices, Impressions

Every time I hear a Christian say *God told me,* I throw up a little bit in my mouth.

Once you lob a *God told me* into a conversation, that should end all debate, right? After all, if God said it, that settles it.

The epitome of this is when prophetic utterances by so called New Apostles are transcribed and then exegeted as if they were on par with Scripture.

If this isn't a delusion from the pit of hell I don't know what is.

"I have a word from God for you."

"I feel that God is speaking this over you."

"I'm getting a word of knowledge right now."

"I just feel that God is saying that you're beautiful."

Spare me your cheap epistemology, please.

Why waste one nanosecond on new revelations, when there is so much authoritative, perfect, old revelation sitting in our Bibles untouched and unexamined?

Itching ears.

The more of God's Word you have hidden in your heart, the more raw material there is for the Spirit of God to apply the Scriptures to your current situation.

This may feel like a revelation, but it is not.

It is the beautiful gift of God's Spirit to the Christian who has devoted their lives to the study of Scripture.

This still small voice is no new revelation. It is, rather, the just-in-time application of the old revelation that we call the Bible, given to those who have bothered to study it. This is properly called illumination, not revelation.

Do you want to hear God's voice?

Open your Bible.

5. Bible-Light

I cannot leave this discussion of cheap epistemology without shining the spotlight on the current trend in preaching to use the Bible as justification for preaching on whatever the preacher wants.

Any motivational speech, any practical how-to guide, any comedy show can be made Christian enough for today's pulpit by adding some Bible verse sprinkles and saying it is from Jesus.

Famous preachers fill sports arenas with their Bible-light cheap epistemology.

The Word of God is a condiment, not the main course.

Nothing in the sermon is regulated by biblical exposition. Nothing is rooted in theology. Nothing adds to the creation of intellectual structures of meaning or shows the interlocking connectedness of all God's truth. Nothing adds a gravitas that will enable listeners to withstand the huffing and puffing of the devil's lies.

The whole thing is a feel good moment, brought to you by a really cool, hip, and fashion-forward preacher.

It is epistemology because it is an approach to the acquisition of truth. It is cheap because it is an impotent counterfeit of the apostolic preaching that turned the world upside down.

I have no doubt I am cementing my status as a really crabby guy. I am sure I'm losing friends by saying these things. Maybe I'm going too far. I hope to God I am not.

Paul's admonition to Timothy applies to all of these modes of cheap epistemology.

> For the time will come when they will not endure sound doctrine, but according to their own desires, because they have itching ears, they will heap up for themselves teachers; and they will turn their ears away from the truth, and be turned aside to fables. (2 Timothy 4:3, 4)

THE B.I.B.L.E. YES THAT'S THE BOOK FOR ME…

Cheap epistemology is like mildew. It grows, it spreads, and it's very hard to get rid of.

But at its core, it is always the same, the exaltation of self, or of Satan, above the invincible all-sufficient Bible.

No experience, encounter, impression, word, emotion, opinion, or fad comes even close to the authority of the propositional truth of Scripture.

For the truly evangelical Christian, the source of truth will always be God's inerrant Word. There is, was, and never will be a substitute for the in-depth teaching of the Word of God, including the patient instruction in the rich vocabulary of theology for all the people of God.

"But we will give ourselves continually to prayer and to the ministry of the Word," the early church apostles said (Acts 6:4).

"No," said the people. "Hang out with us and be our friends and be visionary and make us feel better and give us steps to follow. Practical application, please. Also, get involved, and stay busy for Jesus, shoulder to shoulder with us. And post pious platitudes mixed with family photos of you planting carrots on social media so we can *connect*."

"Okay," said the pastor, "but my sermons will be shorter and more shallow."

"That's all right, as long as they're funny and crammed with stories. Especially vulnerable ones."

Because truth takes a back seat to feelings.

Seminaries tell pastors to "put the cookies on the bottom shelf." They mean to keep it simple because people are dumb.

This view flies in the face of both Scripture and church history.

Jude, writing to the everyday people of God, "...found it necessary to write to you exhorting you to contend earnestly for the faith which was once for all delivered to the saints" (Jude 1:3).

Do not miss that "the faith"—in this context the doctrinal content of Scripture—had been delivered to the *saints*. Not the popes, priests, pastors, or preachers, but to all the people of God. That deposit of theology is the heritage of the pews equally with the pulpit. It is a strategic blunder for pastors to reserve theological meat for church leaders only.

Even more importantly, it is the job of the saints, as custodians of this doctrine, to know it so well they can "earnestly contend for it." They must be so theologically informed they can raise a defense, they can answer critics, they can tear down misconceptions, and correct preconceptions against the truth of God. They can stand toe to toe with atheists, agnostics, postmodernists, modernists, romantics, Hindus, Buddhists, and anyone else who would trash God's Word.

Even when Scripture sounds antiquated, or narrowminded, or ridiculously out of date, it is still where we take our stand.

God has ordained that his truth be diffused throughout the body, not concentrated at the top among leadership.

This is not happening.

And so we have opened the door to chaos.

THE DOGMA IS THE DRAMA

Another prophetic voice from the past, Dorothy Sayers said it best. Way back in the World War Two era, she wrote:

> Official Christianity, of late years, has been having what is known as a bad press. We are constantly assured that the churches are empty because preachers insist too much upon doctrine—dull dogma as people call it. The fact is the precise opposite. It is the neglect of dogma that makes for dullness. The Christian faith is the most exciting drama that ever staggered the imagination of man—and the dogma is the drama.

The dogma, she says—meaning the theological formulations such as those found in the confessions, and in *Basic Christian Doctrines,* is the drama. This is the truly interesting bit.

Sayers continues:

> [T]he cry today is: "Away with the tedious complexities of dogma—let us have the simple spirit of worship; just worship, no matter of what!" The only drawback to this demand for a generalized and undirected worship is the practical difficulty of arousing any sort of enthusiasm for the worship of nothing in particular.

Without a well-formed theology of the nature and attributes of God, we can only send our worship into outer space where it will boomerang off a god of our own creation, made in our own image, and, thus, reflect nothing but an insidious worship of self. Without biblical theology, there is nothing to worship but a reflection of ourselves, the inevitable fruit of cheap epistemology.

Yet every survey shows a stark biblical illiteracy ravishing the Church. Where do we find our truth? Everywhere but the Bible it seems.

I am afraid for the Church.

We – and I mean the Church at large – find ourselves back in idol-saturated Ephesus, worshipping The Unknown God.

> Theologically, this country is at present in a state of utter chaos, established in the name of religious toleration, and rapidly degenerating into the flight from reason and the death of hope. We are not happy in this condition, and there are signs of a very great eagerness, especially among the younger people, to find a creed to which they can give wholehearted adherence. This is the Church's opportunity, if she chooses to take it.[5]

Has there ever been a better descriptor of 21st century culture, and with that of the 21st century church, than those words, "the flight from reason, and the death of hope"?

Cheap epistemology gives birth to irrationality and irrationality gives birth to chaos.

I have so many Bibles, it is easy to take them for granted.

On my good days however I remember that every time I hold the Bible, I am holding a blood-bought, sacrificial gift. I'm holding a monumental miracle of the mercy of God. I'm holding a costly treasure.

"This is the church's opportunity, if she chooses to take it." My words today can only echo Sayers' prescient warnings of a generation past.

May God grant us an army of Pauls to say, "The One whom you worship without knowing, Him I proclaim to you" (Acts 17:23).

Dear Christian, where do you find your truth?

---

1. Carl F.H. Henry, ed. *Basic Christian Doctrines* (Grand Rapids, MI: Baker Book House, 1971.
2. The Awana Youth Association provides Bible-based clubs for boys and girls through churches around the world.
3. Michael Foust, "Seminary President Admits She Doesn't Believe in Heaven, Miracles or Christ's Resurrection." April 25, 2019 in Christian Headlines retrieved April 20, 2020 from https://www.christianheadlines.com/contributors/michael-foust/seminary-president-admits-she-doesn-t-believe-in-heaven-miracles-or-christ-s-resurrection.html
4. Lloyd-Jones, D. Martyn. *Preaching and Preachers* . Zondervan. Kindle Edition. Location 4576.
5. Dorothy Sayers. *Creed or chaos? : why Christians must choose either dogma or disaster (or, why it really does matter what you believe)*. Manchester, NH: Sophia Institute Press, 1999, ©1949, pp. 44, 45.

5 / WOKENESS — THE FELLOWSHIP OF DARKNESS AND LIGHT

THE SOUTHERN BAPTIST convention made news in 2019 by adopting a resolution accepting "Critical Race Theory and Intersectionality" as valid tools in biblical interpretation.[1] To be sure, our Baptist friends hemmed in their acceptance of these controversial tools with strong statements on the supremacy of Scripture and disclaimers about "the misuse of insights gained from critical race theory, intersectionality, and any unbiblical ideologies that emerge from their use..." But in the end, by following a holy impulse to deal with oppression in God-honoring ways, they cracked open the door to an unholy truth-devouring monster.

Even Wikipedia traces the origins of CRT to Marxism.[2] An ardently secular, atheistic philosophy is not of God, no matter how noble its stated aspirations. There can be no fellowship between darkness and light.

I first heard the term "woke" from my daughter. Now, I can't get away from it. The vocabulary of micro-aggressions, privilege, woke, white fragility, problematizing, intersectionality, and a swarm of equally impenetrable verbal sorcery, is the offspring of a decidedly materialist and humanist ideology. Yet the underlying premises of Critical Race Theory and Intersectionality (CRT/I) have been unwittingly swallowed by a gullible church. Indeed, to even question these premises is proof of one's oppressor status.

These are called "analytical tools" but, since when is there an "analytical tool" that stands above analysis?

By all accounts, it is less an analytical tool than it is a philosophy which simply cannot be squared with evangelical theology.

There are tools of construction and tools of destruction. If ever there were a set of tools for destruction, it is the entire kit that comes with CRT/I.

It is, however, dangerously naive to think these tools will stay in the toolbox. No. The tools of CRT/I will wait till the dark of night. Then they will come to life. They will rampage through the home, shattering everything, before turning on their owners and hammering them into a quivering heap cowering in the corner.

Assimilate or perish.

In the end, these tools will beat the Bible to pulp. They will then fashion a shiny new theological golden calf made in the image of an Ivy League professor.

Actually, all this is already happening.

Those who crafted CRT/I have explicitly announced their goal: "revolution."[3]

The Original Sins of racism, sexism, and homo/trans-phobia are baked into the cake of Western Civilization, they say. All these transgressions are part and parcel of law, culture, and government. They are "systemic." These sins animated the founders of America. They are in our founding documents. There is no way to uproot them. The only solution is a complete overthrow of the system, founded upon a complete overhaul, and minute censoring, of language.

Violence in the streets, in the lecture hall, in the sanctuary, and to long cherished doctrines and wisely ordained traditions, is justified in order to compensate for the violence done to intersectional sufferers over the generations.

The goal is revolution. In fact, the stated goal of the practitioners of CRT/I is "to make revolution irresistible."[4]

I am one generally timid guy, at a desk, in front of a laptop, sounding an alarm.

Marxism might also be considered an analytical tool. But it has proven its inability to stay in the toolbox. The consequence continues to be bloody revolution. Look at Hong Kong in 2019. The American riots of 2020. Darwinism, Naziism, Antifa, the Occupy Movement, the shouting down of opposing voices, the "disinviting" of un-woke speakers from the platforms of academia — analytical tools escaping the tool box to batter injustice with injustice.

Analytical tools?

Use at your own risk.

Wokenness is brokenness.

> Woe to those who call evil good, and good evil; Who put darkness for light, and light for darkness; Who put bitter for sweet, and sweet for bitter! (Isaiah 5:20)

THEOLOGICAL INCOMPATIBILITY

Critical Race Theory and Intersectionality are just the latest in an endless stream of philosophies representing the spirit of the age.

These philosophies cannot be reconciled with biblical Christianity.

> Beware lest anyone cheat you through philosophy and empty deceit, according to the tradition of men, according to the basic principles of the world, and not according to Christ. (Colossians 2:8)

I thank God for those who, in the name of Jesus Christ, fight the fight of faith for righteousness and biblical decency in society. Whether they call it "social justice" — a term that is increasingly loaded with political baggage — "social ministry," or just plain old "love," I am on their side.

I am not suggesting for a moment that we should turn a blind eye to our institutional sins. I am not justifying racism, sexism, and cruelty against those whose sexual expressions do not fit the norms in the church. These ecclesiastical sins must be, and continue to be, addressed. I applaud the impulse within the SBC that drove them to adopt Resolution 9. It is a holy impulse to work toward societal righteousness and to address long-standing sins in the church.

But CRT/I is not the tool by which we address them. In fact, the adoption of CRT/I will set us back and aggravate the pre-existing chaos.

The handmaiden of CRT/I commonly called "social justice" wildly distorts biblical teaching on both justice and society.

There is a litany of fundamental incompatibilities between the tools of Critical Race Theory /Intersectionality and Scripture. Let's consider a handful of these incompatibilities.

ORIGINAL SIN

In Scripture, disobedience to God is our original sin. Guilt and corruption have been transmitted down the human family tree.

But in CRT/I, oppression is the original sin. Oppression, by definition, applies only to those in privileged positions of power. Those privileged sinners include every person not identified within an intersectional minority.

In this system, many oppressors don't know they are oppressors. All of this renders intersectional people innocent, untainted by original sin. It identifies oppressors as those who must be silenced — as CRT/I activists would say, "Shut up, listen, and agree."

Furthermore, to define sin as systemic is to rig the system.

Nobody can say anything untainted by sin. No action, however well-intentioned, can be pure. CRT/I puts the church into an unwinnable situation. The power of the Cross is negated, as it may cleanse the heart, but it can never flush the political or cultural system. This becomes the ultimate legalism. CRT/I requires the exhausting climbing of endless ladders of perfection to assuage the implacable demands of the perpetually offended.

Never mind that neither Jesus, nor the apostles, nor his disciples engaged in anything even remotely resembling the protests, power-plays, and pursuit of vengeance characteristic of the CRT/I practitioners of today.

In Scripture, salvation is deliverance from original sin. In CRT/I, salvation is the oppressed rising up to take back power from oppressors, while at the same time, heaping never-ending retribution on their heads. This retribution takes perversely sanctioned forms of scorn, silencing, cancelling, theft of property, smashing windows, looting, shaming, disinviting, shouting down, and even violence. All of this in the name of Jesus?

"Jesus wept."

In fact, there is no salvation for oppressors. They can never eliminate their racism or other -isms, as they are constituent elements of a privileged being. They can never atone for their sins. They can only undertake an endless process of "race work" which turns the tables on the oppressors — a far cry from the grace of our Lord Jesus.

REVELATION

In Scripture, our source of truth is the revelation of God given us in Scripture. But in CRT/I the epistemology is changed. Truth bubbles up from the experience of the oppressed. There can be no questioning of it. There can be no analysis of it, not even by Scripture itself, without compounding our sin. Far from being a tool to analyze Scripture, CRT/I sets itself above Scripture and stands in judgment over it.

In fact, *A Progressive's Style Guide,* which identifies language that must and must not be used by CRT/I advocates, outlaws at least 30 expressions commonly used in Scripture.[5] Unless Scripture is modified to conform with the style guide, it becomes part of the oppressive system.

CRT/I is a new kind of gnosticism. The ancient philosophy of gnosticism glommed onto every religion it touched. It infected Judaism, Christianity, and even pagan religions. It split people into insiders and outsiders, and promised esoteric knowledge to the chosen few. The early church saw it for the deadly dangerous heresy it was, and rooted it out.

In CRT/I, the founders and practitioners have insider status, and access to secret knowledge which cannot be analyzed or questioned. It creates an impenetrable maze of vocabulary and new terminology, incantations of power known only by the magicians of its craft. It creates a pecking order of novices and initiates and shamans and gurus. All of this is a far cry from the priesthood of all believers. All of this is heresy.

HUMAN EXPERIENCE

In Scripture, the dismal lot of humankind is "common" (1 Corinthians 10:13). The rain falls on the just and the unjust. Good things happen to bad people. Bad things happen to good people. Sin has happened to and from and upon and because of all people. We live in a fallen world, and suffering is our *universal* experience.

"For there is no difference... for all have sinned," declares the Lord (Romans 3:23).

"Except for the intersectional victim," declares the Woke. The CRT/I viewpoint creates a difference where God has explicitly declared there is no difference.

Sin is the common lot of humanity. We are, one and all, sin's victims. We are also, one and all, sin's perpetrators. Welcome to the human condition.

Not only is sin common, but so also is suffering.

The trials and tribulations of life are "common to" mankind. You may not have walked in my shoes, but you have walked in your shoes. And your shoes have seen plenty of trouble, just like mine.

And if you have even an ounce of human compassion, you can sympathize with me as I can sympathize with you.

> No temptation [*peirosmos*, trial, trouble, or tough time] has overtaken you except such as is common to man; but God is faithful, who will not allow you to be tempted beyond what you are able, but with the temptation will also make the way of escape, that you may be able to bear it. (1 Corinthians 10:13)

CRT/I takes a hammer to all that, deconstructing it, asserting we have nothing in common, and shoving us all into isolated cubicles of victimhood, where all we can do is snarl at each other, plotting vengeance and demanding reparation at the point of a gun.

SANCTIFICATION

In Scripture, sanctification is achieved as a process of growth in grace in which those formerly called sinners begin to exhibit their new status as saints. In CRT/I, the process is confrontational, in your face, and non-voluntary. It is often shouted, insisted upon, and demanded, NOW. It arises from bitterness, not love. Vengeance, not forgiveness. Coercive powers of government or academia, not growth in grace. It formalizes the airing of grievances, creating an unholy mess.

Sanctification is morphed into a power-play. Its dynamics represent the opposite of a Savior who never confronted the institutions of government, academia, or religion. Yes, he turned over tables in his Father's house, but to purify his church from greedy moneychangers, not to incite revolution.

How can Paul's power-encounter with the then reigning high priest be in any way reconciled with the tenets of CRT/I?

> Then Paul said to him, "God will strike you, you whitewashed wall! For you sit to judge me according to the law, and do you command me to be struck contrary to the law?" And those who stood by said, "Do you revile God's high priest?" Then Paul said, "I did not know, brethren, that he was the high priest; for it is written, 'You shall not speak evil of a ruler of your people.'" (Acts 23:3-5)

Isn't this the opposite of "speaking truth to power?"

Neither Jesus, nor his apostles, can ever be shown to have been using tools anywhere resembling CRT/I, though they had plenty of opportunities to do so.

UNITY

In Scripture, we see the revolutionary power of the gospel at work, as rich and poor, slave and free, male and female, were joined together at the same table to share the Lord's Supper. God, by grace, has done the unthinkable: he has redeemed by his blood a united church, "Out of every tribe and tongue and people and nation" (Revelation 5:9).

He has brought into being a new spiritual species in which, "There is neither Jew nor Greek, there is neither slave nor free, there is neither male nor female; for you are all one in Christ Jesus" (Galatians 3:28).

In stark and diabolical contrast, CRT/I shatters the unity of the church in favor of a hard-edged tribalism, rooted in victim-hood, adjudged by language-police, enforced by violence, and overcome by— well, there is no overcoming these tribal distinctions. There is only the endless airing of grievances, coupled with an equally endless shaming of the unatonable sins of privilege.

The Cross is denuded of power, the church is reduced to

endless squabbles and self-shaming, the gospel is exchanged for social justice, and we all back into our corners to fight over who is more offended.

THE KINGDOM

In Scripture, the eschatological ideal is achieved when Jesus himself returns to establish his rule and reign in our lives and our world. But in CRT/I the eschatological ideal is economic and political power, concentrated in the hands of gnostic insiders who know what's best for all.

Paul asked, "What communion has light with darkness?" There are some entities that are simply incompatible, irreconcilable, and — like matter and anti-matter — reciprocally destructive.

So it is with biblical interpretation and the tools of Critical Race Theory and Intersectionality.

God help us.

Chaos.

BE IT RESOLVED

May I respectfully offer a new resolution for my friends in the Southern Baptist Convention. Following the pattern of Resolution 9, I offer these...

Whereas Scripture paints the hopeful picture of every tongue, tribe, and nation gathered as one around the throne of the Lamb, and

Whereas Paul describes the beautiful hope of human unity in a church where, "There is neither Jew nor Greek, there is neither slave nor free, there is neither male nor female; for you are all one in Christ Jesus" (Galatians 3:28), and

Whereas Scripture condemns all under sin, and declares, "there is no difference" (Romans 3:22,23), and

Whereas Christ died for all and offers salvation to all without exception, and

Whereas Jesus ministered to wealthy oppressors, religious oppressors, and political oppressors, as well as to the oppressed, thus equalizing everybody in the sight of God, and

Whereas the tools of biblical hermeneutics and analysis that have evolved over thousands of years have proven to be adequate for the task insofar as they reflect the hermeneutics of the biblical authors themselves, and

Whereas Scripture is not only inspired and inerrant, but also sufficient for every day and age including our own, and

Whereas the Word of God possesses sanctifying power,[6] and the Church is called to impact society for biblical righteousness by the power of sanctified living, and speaking out, and

Whereas Christians both in positions of privilege and in positions of oppression are called to humble themselves, to repent, and to make amends for their own sins, not those of distant ancestors, and

Whereas historic evangelical Christianity has done the greatest good in human history for people who have been marginalized by society, therefore

BE IT RESOLVED that the identity politics, hard-edged tribalism, irredeemability of some, and revolution advocated by the ideology of CRT/I have no place in the thinking or processes of Christian truth and the church, and

BE IT RESOLVED that the people of God continue to grow in grace and holiness, so that they may love their neighbors — regardless of tribal affiliation or systemic infection — and work and speak for biblical righteousness in society by the power of divine grace, according to the examples of Christ and his apostles.

---

1. Resolution 9, "On Critical Race Theory and Intersectionality," Birmingham, AL, 2019 at http://www.sbc.net/resolutions/2308/resolution-9--on-critical-race-theory-and-intersectionality, retrieved November 17, 2019.
2. Retrieved October 12, 2020.

3. Toni Cade Bambara, quoted in "Style Matters - Sum of Us's new progressive style guide," July 19, 2016, at Resource Media, at http://www.resource-media.org/style-matters-sum-uss-new-progressive-style-guide/ retrieved, November 17, 2019.

4. *Ibid.*

5. Hanna Thomas and Anna Hirsch, "A Progressive's Style Guide" at http://interactioninstitute.org/wp-content/uploads/2016/06/Sum-Of-Us-Progressive-Style-Guide.pdf, retrieved November 17, 2019.

6. John 17:17, Acts 20:32.

THERE IS A CATEGORY of books in the Christian marketplace called "Christian Life." The category spans sixteen sub-categories: General; Death, Grief, Bereavement; Devotional; Family; Inspirational; Love and Marriage; Men's Issues; Personal Growth; Prayer; Professional Growth; Relationships; Social Issues; Spiritual Growth; Spiritual Warfare; Stewardship and Giving; and Women's Issues. Each subcategory itself can be subdivided further. Publishers call these BISAC codes and you can Google them. You'll also find them on the back cover of your book, right by the barcode.

Every Christian Life book published will be slotted into one of these categories.

We could say the same for every sermon ever preached on the Christian life.

And for every song ever sung, and every small group ever gathered, and every website, podcast, and blog ever posted.

If we are writing, singing, speaking, or posting about any aspect of everyday life for the child of God, we find ourselves in the category the publishing world calls Christian Life.

Theology offers another name for the category: Sanctification.

In 1875, evangelical Christians first gathered in a British

city called Keswick for a Bible conference (the w is silent, *Kezzik*). The Keswick Convention has continued without break for more than 140 years. Thousands of Christians have gathered through the years to enjoy holiday, and to hear dynamic preaching of God's Word.

For much of the Keswick Convention's history, the preaching promoted a particular view of sanctification that came to be called Keswick Sanctification. It's also been called Victorious Christian Living, and the Higher Life Movement.

This view emphasized that just as salvation was by grace through faith, so also our post-conversion Christian life is by grace through faith. We didn't shift from grace to works at salvation; it is by grace, through faith alone, forever. In addition, Keswick Sanctification emphasized the indispensable role of the Holy Spirit in our everyday holiness.

An evangelical panoply, including the likes of Billy Graham, D.L. Moody, R.A. Torrey, A.B. Simpson, and hosts of others, were influenced by this convention.

My point is not to advocate for a Keswick theology of sanctification.

My point is to remind us that for a good half century, Christians gathered by the tens of thousands to hear preaching on the topic of – wait for it – sanctification. This was a sanctification conference.

A.K.A. Holiness.

When was the last time there was a national conference of note on holiness? Is there even a market for that?

J.I. Packer said, "there is need to blow the whistle on the sidelining of personal holiness that has been a general trend among Bible-centered Western Christians during my years of ministry."[1]

Can I get an Amen?

HOW DOES GOD CHANGE A LIFE?

If surveys are right, odds are strong only a wispy minority of Christians could offer up a halfway decent definition of what sanctification means. Herein lies our tragedy. It is not simply that we don't know what sanctification means. Nor is it that we – the Church – by losing an idea of sanctification, have set ourselves on the precipice of moral failure and unholy accommodationism. The greatest tragedy is that we have lost sight of any coherent theory whatsoever as to *how God changes lives and the power by which he does it.*

Our deepest problem is that every author, preacher, songwriter, and YouTuber dealing with any topic in the Christian Life realm is, by definition, promoting a particular *theological* viewpoint on sanctification.

But most don't even know it.

Is your book on Men's Issues or Women's Issues? You are writing about sanctification.

Does your podcast focus on Marriage and Family from a biblical perspective? Adoption? Arts and Entertainment? Love languages? You are podcasting on sanctification.

Will a hundred thousand subscribers view your YouTube videos on finances and generosity from God's perspective? You are proclaiming a central aspect of sanctification.

What about social justice? Racial harmony? Decency in civil discourse? These are, one and all, aspects of sanctification.

The problem is that not even one in a hundred preachers and authors and online personalities has bothered to articulate their particular persuasion on how God makes people holy, i.e., they have not landed their own theology of sanctification.

I doubt they have even thought about it.

So all they can do is offer practical advice, divorced from the power of God. A litany of imperatives. Do this, and then that, and then the next thing, and your marriage/dating/ finances/ physical health/happiness quotient/depression will all be fixed. Steps. Recipes. Action items. To Do Lists. Duties.

Obligations. Preachers call them "practical applications." Paul called it "Having a form of godliness, but denying its power" (2 Timothy 3:5).

Even worse, we end up getting into a colossal tug of war over the big issues of the day. Yes, racism is a huge problem in the church. So is sexism. So is pre-marital sex. So are a million other things. How do we address them?

Either we will wrestle over the reins of coercive power to get our way, or we will guide the church into a process of holiness.

We can't do both.

When we deal with the heart, we are dealing with sanctification. When we deal with behavior only, we have become everything Jesus blasted.

We are suffering the Pharisaical Captivity of the Church.

The unalterable truth remains: absolutely nothing in the Christian Life moves forward God's way unless it is imbued with God's power.

It is a coherent doctrine of sanctification alone that shows precisely how to tap into God's power. Far too many books, too many sermons, too many websites, too many podcasts, too many everythings, tell us what to do, but never tell us how to do it *by the power of God.*

We've lapsed into a chaotic unsanctified jumble—very busy for Jesus, and always on the verge of burnout. It is rampant legalism. God's work done God's way must employ God's power. But we don't know how. So the devil laughs at us. The world ignores us. Godless people are weary of us. And we congratulate ourselves inside our own Christian bubbles.

Isn't this a mess?

THREE VIEWS

J.I. Packer has done the Church a huge favor by outlining three common theological approaches to sanctification in his classic work, *Keep In Step With The Spirit.*[2]

1. *Augustinianism*, which is adopted by the majority of Reformed churches. Augustinianism promotes sanctification by the power of God's Spirit and grace, coupled with our faithful life of struggle.

"Miserable sinner sanctification," as B.B. Warfield called it. He did not mean this in a neurotic sense, but in the sense that we will never stop needing God's mercy and grace.

Sanctification under this view becomes "God-dependent effort" under "sustained obedience." In other words, it's holiness through a kind of struggle sustained by God.

2. *Wesleyanism*, also called *perfectionism* or *entire sanctification*, is holiness through a dramatic experience of divine love. In this "second work of grace," the sin nature is eradicated, and the believer is enabled to live an essentially sinless life.

Packer suggests it is "Augustinianism augmented rather than abandoned" (p. 110). It results in an entirely sanctified life. To Packer, this view gave Christian living a "quality of ardor, exuberance, and joy... that went beyond anything we find in Calvin, the Puritans, and the earlier Pietists [i.e., in the Augustinians]" (p. 134).

I roomed with a pastor of this persuasion while pursuing my doctorate. He claimed in full sincerity that he had not sinned at all since his sanctification-experience many years prior. As his roommate, I had ample opportunity to test his claim, but those stories must remain locked within a vault of confidentiality.

3. *Keswick Teaching* was a modification of Wesleyanism, and popularized by the famous Keswick Convention mentioned above. Keswick sanctification rescues holiness from legalism by declaring it to be just as much "by grace through faith" as is salvation. It offers effortless holiness, not by striving, but by faith.

Packer goes on to point out pros and cons of each viewpoint, and in the end advocates for the Augustinian position.

I'm a Keswickian, myself, with a modification. Whereas classical Keswick sanctification portrays the route to holiness as an effortless move of God—less like climbing an Augustinian stairway and more like riding a Keswickian elevator—I would quibble over the effortlessness of it. Yes, it's holiness by faith, *but such faith is a mighty struggle.* I would rather have Christians *struggle to* believe God's promises than *struggle against* sin. Win the battle of faith, and every other victory falls into place. Including sanctification.

Faith is the victory.

PLEASE PICK ONE

My point is not to advocate for any particular sanctification viewpoint. My point is to suggest that every Christian in a position of influence pick one. Any one. It doesn't matter which one, as God has worked mightily through them all.

Just please pick one. Master it. Learn its details. Find its scriptural basis. Wear out the pages of God's Word to develop it. And then keep everything you say consistent with it. Steep your heart in sanctification by the power of God. He is *Yahweh M'qaddesh,* the Lord Who Sanctifies. Know him well by this name.

Pick a perspective on sanctification, master it, and then, for the love of all that's holy, promote it in everything you preach, write, exhort, or post.

How?

It's simple really.

Create despair.

Create hopeful despair. "What I'm about to tell you to do is humanly impossible, but with God, all things are possible." Despair of self and hope in Christ. That's the supernatural formula cutting across all these sanctifying theories. Remind your people only God can transform their lives, and then promise them he will.

Beat the drum incessantly: "Not I, but Christ."

Not I.

But Christ.

This is the only way to overcome our stunted condition. It's the only way to become whole. Holy. Wholesome.

It is the only God-given, divinely-empowered way to clean out the moral chaos in our churches.

Sanctification creates radiant Christ-bearers.

I'm pleading with every author, speaker, preacher, teacher, podcaster, video producer, blogger, and communicator of anything remotely Christian – for the love of Christ, nail down a Scripture-taught, grace-based, God-powered position on sanctification, and let every syllable you publish stay consistent with it.

When we go back to setting every aspect of the Christian Life into the context of a full-orbed doctrine of sanctification, the devil will shed his acid tears, and the world will take notice of us. "We've never seen people like this before. Why are they so different?"

Christ-in-us will shine through.

That alone is the singular difference a lost world most urgently needs to see.

----

1. In *Rediscovering Holiness: Know the Fullness of Life in God* (Ann Arbor, MI: Vine Books, 1992).
2. J.I. Packer, *Keep In Step With the Spirit* (Grand Rapids: Revell) 1984 in ch. 4, "Mapping the Spirit's Path," pp. 121-169.

Nobody riled up Jesus like legalists. But the problem then, as it is today, is that legalists don't know they're legalists. And even when Jesus told them so, they had the temerity to argue back.

It's not that we are legalists, they argued. It's that you, Jesus, are a bottom-feeding antinomian.

There never was a legalist that 'fessed up without a major whack upside the head.

Witness Paul on the road to Damascus. Or Peter after the vision of the sheets.

The human heart is hopelessly addicted to impressing God in its own strength. But this is impossible. Jesus said so: "With humans it is impossible" (Mark 10:27).

I won't go into the whole case for grace, as I have written a trilogy of books on this most glorious theme. It will be more helpful to explore some subtle ways the evangelical church has constituted itself around legalism, and doesn't even know it.

WHAT SHALL WE TEACH THE KIDS?

As a novice pastor, I had the enormous benefit of rubbing shoulders with some giants of the faith. Lance B. Latham was the revered founder of Awana (a worldwide Bible memory club for kids) and Camp Awana. By the time I joined the staff of the church he founded, he was retired. Doc, as we called him, looked to be about 300 years old. But there was strength in his handshake and a sparkle in his crystal-blue eyes. He still kept office hours at the church. He was a living legend and a hero to countless thousands of kids who grew up through Awana.

As the leader of Awana clubs in the church he founded, I had the incredible privilege of benefiting from Doc's mentorship. When I asked him once what to teach the children in our clubs, he didn't hesitate. "Teach them their riches in Christ," he said.

That was decades ago, and I have never budged from this simple wisdom.

I have spent the bulk of my ministry life, however, lamenting the scarcity of this kind of thinking.

I would argue, in Christian love, that most children's curriculum constitutes institutionalized legalism. What else can it be when we offer endless lessons about sharing and character? What else is it when we continually shove behavioral lessons down vulnerable kids' throats, like a robin shoving worm-bits down its hatchlings' gullets? Be nice. Obey. Share. Tell the truth. Sit still.

What are we, dog trainers?

We possess an invincible God, an incomparable gospel, and an invaluable mission. We possess riches to last a lifetime — enough positive affirmations to establish a young soul on a theological rock that will support their psychological health forever.

Let's teach that.

Let's lay out a feast of who God is. Let's feed them who Christ is, and what he has done. Let's walk them through a bloody Old Testament sacrifice, and show them how each minute detail points to Christ. Let's wear a priest's ephod, and show how each gem sparkles with the radiance of who God has designed them to be. Let's build a giant fish and have it swallow a prophet who resents grace.

Let's teach them theology.

Let's serve up the whole counsel of God.

Let's teach them the wonders of a grace so deep the devil can't uproot it.

Build a temple and show them the laver, that they might feel washed white as snow. Paint it glittering gold, that we might slather their imaginations with a God glorious beyond words.

And let us, please, teach them the big words. The majestic vocabulary of faith.

The best car mechanics grew up tinkering under the hood with their parents or older siblings. At age eight, they could change the oil. By age nine, they were changing the belts. When they were twelve, they rebuilt a carburetor. When they were fifteen, they learned about fuel injection. At twenty five they can diagnose your engine problem before you pop the hood.

Let's make our kids their own mechanics for their own souls. My point here is twofold: a) They grew up that way. Just as Jewish children grew up with Sabbaths and sacrifices and burnt offerings and priests, all shadows of Christ. It took decades to build these truths into their hearts. b) They learned the technical vocabulary early on. A nine year old can understand propitiation and immutability just fine, and they will remember them forever, because they learned the words while their brains were still malleable.

But my deeper point brings us back to legalism.

LEGALISM

Unless we are instilling within them the massive truth-structures of grace and faith, our kids grow up thinking Christianity is just a system of morals — out of date morals at that. As soon as they have their independence, they will jettison the morals, and Christfianity with it.

They have learned some moral fables but have never learned grace. They have never discovered that Christianity is predominantly about what God has done for us. They are convinced it's about what we must do for God. That's where Moralistic Therapeutic Deism invariably leads.

There's the legalism.

Stop it.

They have never explored the wonders of an interlocking truth-system so majestic it can take our breath away. It's massive. It's a huge lego-like edifice of truth meshing with truth to create a whole-world truth-claim that comprehends everything they will ever study anywhere. But they don't even know it exists. They don't see math class locked up in God's wondrous creation, or psychology class discovering, as if new, the ancient truths of Scriptures. Church has offered nothing deep for them, and so nothing transcendent, and therefore not enough mystery to keep them interested past junior high.

Behavioral imperatives always become annoying once hormones kick in.

Stop it.

Our kids have never linked their fragile identities with the almighty declarations of God as to who they really are. We have not taught them. Instead, we have flogged them. We are Pharaoh's taskmasters, demanding they make behavioral bricks without theological straw.

Our kids do not know the psychological benefits of saying, "I am righteous, I am holy, I am beloved, I have dominion, I have access, I am forgiven, I am rich beyond compare, I am destined for glory, I have a purpose, I am one of a kind, I am blessed, I am justified, I am sanctified, I am redeemed, I am a saint, I am secure forever, I am in Christ, I am nobody's victim, I possess a glory that will one day dazzle the angels..." and on and on.

But they know they're supposed to share their loaves and fish.

Stunted.

So they limp beneath their royal identities as children of God, and become easy prey for a seductive *cosmos diabolicus.* Yes, it is the devil's world, and he's eating Christian kids for lunch every single day.

Stop it.

Teach them their riches in Christ.

I'm making the case that the culprit is legalism embedded in the very philosophies that guide our teaching of children. It's even embedded in the teachers. Moses told parents to teach their kids everything all the time. Let's do the same.

Show them *propitiation*, and they will have a foundation for knowing exactly how and why God is satisfied with them.

Embed the truths of *justification* in their tender psyches, so they can live with a sense of having nothing left to prove.

Paint a thousand pictures of *redemption*, so they have the seeds of freedom implanted early enough to ward off addictions and dysfunctions that would put them back in chains.

Magnify *omnipotence*, so they know what it feels like to worship a God who can puff out a universe and all the complexities within it.

And yes, teach them not only the concepts, but the words. Why? Because the words are the containers for the ideas. They are the only containers. The words keep us from thinking the whole thing is a disconnected jumble.

Redemption is redemption, whether it's Moses at the Red Sea, or Jesus' blood at the point of your addiction. It's all connected.

Be sure to connect the dots between the truths you teach and the Bible verses that teach them, so they can clobber the devil with Bible verses when he comes to suck out their souls.

Wait a minute.

It just hit me that everything I've said about children's ministry can also apply to adults.

So I'll just leave it at that.

As for me and my house, we will revel in the wonders of an

illimitable God and the majestic edifice of truth that flows from his grace-filled heart. And we will luxuriate in the riches of divine grace till we have our heads on straight enough to point everyone we know to the treasure we found when we found Christ.

I GREW UP IN AN ERA of unrestrained Second Coming Mania. Jack Van Impe made me believe I'd never see my junior year of high school. The seventies classic, *A Thief In The Night*, scared the hell out of me and a bunch of my peers. Complex wall charts of Bible prophecy adorned the churches I frequented. Before Jerry Jenkins and Tim LaHaye struck a nerve with the *Left Behind* series, Hal Lindsey scared us all with *The Late, Great Planet Earth*.

Every nuclear warhead lent credence to the idea that Jesus would come again any day now. We did mock "Rapture Drills" (jumping in the air). When we said our goodbyes, we often said, "Here, there, or in the air."

Camps and youth groups sang *I Wish We'd All Been Ready*, and we were. We were pre-trib, and pre-mil, and ready to meet our Maker. Daniel's ten toes were going to come together—the European Common Market, something we Christians foresaw twenty years before it happened—and the Mark of the Beast was on its way. There was Bible prophecy in the air, and you could smell it.

But something happened.

The church burned out on Bible prophecy.

No more books. No more conferences. No more singing

about it. It is as if we collectively underwent an eschatology-appendectomy.

When we did, a shift so subtle took place we barely noticed.

THE SHIFT

The evangelical church in America, which had been fervently pre-millennial, evolved into a "whatever-millennial" position, and from there—thanks to the now-defunct emerging church movement, and a thousand other outlets—she has *drifted into* a functionally post-millennial theological position.

Which means that to say "Jesus is coming" within a contemporary evangelical culture means he's coming right now to heal that tumor, knock you over, or break that addiction.

"Wow, God really showed up today."

"Heaven comes to earth."

"King of Heaven, come now."

Into the vacuum created when prophecy-mania went away, flowed a realized eschatology that, to mess with yesterday's phrase, is so earthly minded it's no heavenly good.

I call it *functional* post-millennialism because the institution's doctrinal statements might still proclaim pre-millennialism, though compared to yesteryear, nobody's talking about a future tense kingdom of Christ.

Instead, we are paying it forward and giving it back, and Jesus is "showing up" by our love here and now, today. If Jesus is "Coming Again," it's not in some kind of apocalyptic fury but only for Saturday's midnight worship gathering, don't miss it.

We are stuck in Groundhog Day, fighting again the fundamentalist/modernist battles of the nineteenth and twentieth centuries. The kingdom of God is not future, but present, or so we are told. It is not so much the rule and reign of Jesus Christ in bodily form at his second advent, but his spiritual reign in our hearts and society today. It is not a dramatic interruption in history, but a gradual infiltration of society, bringing love to the world and to its institutions.

Why look forward to a future heaven when you can bring heaven to earth now?

I am suggesting that an eschatological heaven has been buried beneath a) an avalanche of signs and wonders on earth, or b) the political/social transformation of earth by doing good, hopefully in Jesus' name, or c) a tidal wave of emotion pursued with a junkie's fervor.

In any case, the radical disjunction between heaven and earth is lost, and with it, the heartfelt longing for something far better than this worn out planet can offer. D.A. Carson saw it coming decades ago:

> My impression, however, is that in many churches Christian assurance is not a major topic for sermons or discussion groups, largely because popular eschatology has become so realized that there is very little futurist element left, except at the merely creedal level. If we do not long for the consummation of our salvation in the new heaven and the new earth, for the *visio Dei* that is the believer's inheritance, then there is little point in talking about our assurance of gaining it. [1]

Who needs salvation if heaven tomorrow is a question mark? And who needs heaven tomorrow when I can have a decent amount of heaven today?

Post-millennialism makes the church optimistic about the world. We can fix it. We can bring about justice and equity for all. We can heal our broken institutions. We can usher in the Lord's return. We can usher in the kingdom of God, here and now, by doing good and by love. Let's go! Let's heal the world's wounds!

As the old hymn says, "With deeds of love and mercy / The heavenly kingdom comes."[2]

It sounds so good.

It's positively inspirational.

Who doesn't want heaven to invade earth, right now?

Who doesn't want Utopia?

Well I don't—not if it is made by even the most well-meaning humans apart from the personal, bodily, eschatological presence of the Lord Jesus Christ. Anyone else at the helm is simply a tyrant with a smile.

This world is, was, and always will be *cosmos diabolicus*, the devil's world. That dark lord owns the world-system, and all we can do is tinker at the fringes.

- Satan is the god of this age (2 Corinthians 4:4).
- He is the prince of the power of the air (Ephesians 2:2).
- The whole world-system lies under his sway (1 John 5:19).

We are easy prey for the Angel of Darkness masquerading as the Angel of Light (2 Corinthians 11:14). All too often, the reforms advocated by well-meaning people, Christians included, create more harm than good. The devil has his fork stuck in all the systems of the world, and no amount of social justice or signs and wonders will pry it out.

We simply can't bring in the Kingdom till the King comes back in glory.

GOOD AND EVIL

The immature Christian lacks the ability to discern good from evil. What God calls evil looks good and *vice versa*. The Author of Hebrews warned against the dangers of such stunted growth:

> But solid food belongs to those who are of full age, that is, those who by reason of use have their senses exercised to discern both good and evil. (Hebrews 5:14)

For the pre-millennialist, the post-millennialist is naively optimistic. Yes, the pre-millennialist is admittedly pessimistic about the culture.

We are not going to create the kingdom now. Give up that dream already. Only King Jesus can heal the world's wounds. Only Jesus, personally present in his physical body, can usher in the kingdom of God. Until that day, until that Millennium, this fallen world is a morally broken pain machine, and we can't fix it.

And the more we try, the more chaos we create.

We can only learn, by the power of God's Word and God's Spirit, to thrive within the pain machine, while we eagerly await the Second Coming of the Lord.

It's a healthy pessimism, with strong biblical roots.

While I am a strong advocate for premillennialism and the pessimism it spawns, it is not without its problems. Sometimes, we detach too soon from the heartbreaks of society. Because we basically have given up on the world, we pull out of the world. The kind of separation that gave birth to skorts and nerdy home-schooled kids (in the past – I'm not criticizing, we home-schooled our kids for many years and they are not nerdy) has the effect of pulling the salt out of the earth, the moral preservative out of society. We largely evacuated education, media, arts, entertainment, and government, and the results are catastrophic in every category.

If we can't fix it, why bother? Or so the idea goes.

It's a fair question.

We bother because Jesus declared us the salt of the earth (Matthew 5:13). We bother because certain qualities of God's future kingdom can indeed be brought into the present today. Paul enumerates a few for us: "For the kingdom of God is not eating and drinking, but righteousness and peace and joy in the Holy Spirit" (Romans 14:17). He adds "power" in 1 Corinthians 4:20. When we live as effective conduits of the grace of God, the world is a better place.

But it is not and cannot be a perfect place.

Heaven cannot be brought to earth. It cannot be reconstructed, approximated, or imitated. Until Jesus returns, this fallen world remains a morally broken pain machine.

We change the world, therefore, by evangelism above all else. Changed hearts, that's what we need. Moms and dads and boys and girls with the Spirit of God, learning the Word of God. That's the ticket. Without evangelism, everything else is whitewashing the devil's world.

Post-millennialism offers a grand distraction from the great mission of evangelism. It diverts dollars and resources from telling the gospel to fixing society.

DOMINIONISM

There is a teaching rising among evangelicals that meshes perfectly with this post-millennial approach. It is called Dominionism. Here is a definition:

> Dominionism is the theocratic idea that regardless of theological view, means, or timetable, Christians are called by God to exercise dominion over every aspect of society by taking control of political and cultural institutions.[3]

There is some debate over its origins. Some suggest, Bill Bright, others Francis Schaeffer, and others Loren Cunningham. Any of these names would most certainly enroll these spheres into the service of evangelism.

But dominionism, as construed today, does not.

The viewpoint teaches there are seven spheres of influence in which Christians must regain dominion. These seven spheres are also called mountains or realms.

The seven realms are arts and entertainment, business, education, family, government, media, and religion.

When we have regained dominion in these realms, we will have ushered in the kingdom of God, or so the idea goes.

I am all for Christians being involved in all of these realms.

This is a great social agenda for the church. But there is one glaring problem. Since when is a social agenda the main thing for the body of Christ?

It seems the only way to regain Dominion in these realms, is to sacrifice the one realm that is the subject of our Lord's Great Commission, i.e., evangelism.

I am not the first one to draw this conclusion.

A famous, old-time evangelist, Paul Rader, spoke these highly controversial words to a gathering of my own denomination – the Christian and Missionary Alliance — in 1913. I quote at length, because the words are so antithetical to the thinking of today, and it's worth considering how dramatically our values have changed over the last century.

> At every open door in the mission field soon will be found great so-called Christian powers and programs of education and reformation to substitute for evangelization and salvation.
>
> The enemy [the devil and his allies] will advance and is advancing their civilization propaganda to laugh out of the trenches the truth of salvation. Hospitals, splendid as they are and benevolent as are their open doors of human kindly service, will be used by the enemy as a substitute for holiness. This camouflage hospital ship, loaded with needed salve, will be anchored in great mission center harbors as a forerunner of salvation along with school buildings. Then like a tape worm these two enterprises will take all the time, strength and money of the missionaries and mission boards.
>
> The enemy slips salvation on a side seat, softly saying, "Sit still, sweet Gospel Story, we're opening the way so you can sing your song very soon."
>
> The "preparation" for the Gospel propaganda is being very successfully used by the enemy everywhere even now. It is high time we recognized this deviating of our men and money by the enemy and believe afresh that the Gospel preached in any tongue, under any circumstance, to any

people has within itself its own dynamite to open its own way.

The Gospel of Jesus Christ does not have to play second fiddle to any hospital, school or civilizing scheme. The Gospel is God's great pioneer. It opens the path, it plows the furrows, it plants the seed. Then the hospitals, schools and civilizing, uplifting schemes come on behind.[4]

It is neither "civilizing schemes," nor gaining Dominion in each of the seven realms that will truly change our world.

No amount of societal dominion can transform the human heart. That requires the miracle of salvation, which in turn requires a laser-beam focus on world and local evangelization. To whatever degree we are turning our attention to other priorities, we are sacrificing this greatest of all commissions to the church.

The gospel is the power of God. The gospel is the message of a Savior, of redeeming blood, and a "so great" salvation coupled with an invitation to believe on him and be saved.

Go into all the world and preach it. Go issue the summons. Call the world to the Savior. Don't skip anybody. And while you call them, deliver them from harm, feed them, clothe them, shelter them, teach them, love them, effect policy change in government, but always in the hopes of getting lost people saved.

Go get people saved and love them as you do it. If we don't, and Jesus comes today, they won't be ready. They'll be left behind.

Evangelism is the closest we'll get to bringing heaven to earth until Jesus returns. Until then, our minds are set on things above, and we eagerly await for our Coming King's return.

"Let us consider this settled," wrote Calvin, "that no one has made progress in the school of Christ who does not joyfully await the day of death and final resurrection."[5]

Amen.

1. D.A. Carson, "Reflections on Christian Assurance" *WTJ* 54 (1992) 1-29.
2. Ernest W. Shurtleff, "Lead On, O King Eternal," public domain, 1887.
3. Frederick Clarkson. "Dominionism Rising: Atheocratic movement hiding in plain sight" Summer 2016, retrieved April 2020 from https://www.politicalresearch.org/2016/08/18/dominionism-rising-a-theocratic-movement-hiding-in-plain-sight.
4. Paul Rader in "The President's Report" to the General Council of the Christian and Missionary Alliance (1912-1913).
5. *Institutes*, 3.10.5.

FIRST IT WAS "EVANGELISM" and "follow up." Then the two were melded into *discipleship*. We've been a bunch of legalists ever since.

Fact: the word *discipleship* never occurs in the Bible. We have *disciples* as a noun, and *making disciples* as a verb, but never discipleship as a title for a theological category or process.

Fact: neither the word disciple nor any of its cognates ever occurs in the epistles.

Fact: the underlying Greek word, *mathetes* (math-AY-tace), means a learner or pupil in the academy. It emphasizes the instructional aspect of spiritual growth.

Discipleship has come to mean so many things, it now means nothing, except, perhaps, for the nebulous machinery for pumping out good, self-sacrificing "Christ-followers." The same could probably be said for a dozen other words in the Christian vocabulary, but this one has a particularly strong influence. It has usurped the role as the main thing the church does. In so doing, it has toppled salvation and enthroned an undefined sanctification as the ruling power.

I would argue that the emphasis on discipleship has murdered evangelism. Before this emphasis, churches trained their people in evangelism. We all knew the Romans Road.

Most of us went through *Evangelism Explosion*. We carried around the *Four Spiritual Laws* and handed out tracts.

Regardless of the fruit, at least our hearts were in the right place.

Now, all of that is dead.

Evangelists, like the late Billy Graham, and Luis Palau, now carry the months-long burden of building "discipleship" programs in local churches before they can come and preach the gospel.

No wonder the age of the evangelist, at least in America, has waned. We're piling discipleship on the evangelist's shoulders, and the result has been the near extinction of the evangelist as a species.

At least the devil is happy.

I frequently preach the gospel and see people saved. When I celebrate this moment on social media, I can bet real money that well-meaning Christians will immediately comment how important it is for them to be discipled so they can demonstrate genuine "life-change."

Shut up.

A birth has just happened. Can't we celebrate the moment? A baby is born! Can't we revel in the greatest miracle of all for even one minute before we start talking about nutrition and college degrees and all that?

They're afraid the gospel doesn't work. They're skeptical. Unless there's "life-change" they weren't really saved, they think.

Again, shut up, in Christian love.

On the Day of Pentecost, three thousand people were saved. The church celebrated. How? By recording the moment in Scripture – including a numerical count – and by immediately baptizing these new converts. No life-change in sight. Just a profession of faith alone in Christ alone, and it's time for the ordinance of baptism.

There's not a whiff of a suggestion that the church should wait to see if their salvation actually "took hold" before baptizing them. Not a whisper of concern that the church might be giving them a "false confidence" by acceding to their salvation-claim in the ordinance of baptism.

"Did you believe in Jesus as your only hope?"

"Yes."

"Great! Welcome to God's family. You're in. Go get dunked."

How irresponsible!

May I suggest that our grandparents' generation had it right. They had it right because they had the terminology right. Correct vocabulary has a way of producing correct thinking.

Evangelism first, and then follow-up. Those were the terms typically used.

These are discrete, albeit related, categories. They can't be merged. The message of the duties of the Christian life always pollutes the message of the gospel of free grace. No matter how many qualifiers you add, the unregenerate mind simply can't separate them. Nobody is saved by being a better person. It is salvation alone that awakens that potentiality. Discipleship, by conflating evangelism with follow-up, produces an invariably legalistic gospel and an invariably confused church.

What God has rent asunder (salvation and obedience), let no one join together.

FULLY DEVOTED WHAT?

It was Willow Creek that coined the phrase, "fully devoted followers of Christ" as a motto for discipleship. About a billion other churches have followed in lockstep.

It's a beautiful phrase, I suppose, and it has served us well enough.

But these days, I throw up a little in my mouth every time I hear it. It has become cliché. Even more, however, I long for the church to flip this perspective on its head.

Let us break it down.

Fully. One hundred percent, completely, without reservation, and without limitation.

Devoted. Dedicated to the point of sacrifice. All in.

Follower. In this context, it means "one who obeys."

Creating fully devoted followers has now become the operating system of the church at large, however the mission may be phrased. This operating system has broad ramifications, at least three of which are, in my opinion, deadly dangerous to the true mission of the church.

First, it is supremely behavioral.

Second, it is utterly human-centered.

Third, it bypasses the biblical priority altogether.

I am suggesting that by defining discipleship this way, and by making it central, we have created a behavior-obsessed, human-centered church. Instead of proclaiming an immutable God and his everlasting gospel, our focus has shifted to behavior modification and collateral techniques.

It's time to flip the "fully-devoted" meme on its head.

What if we were so gospel-wise, and grace-oriented we made it our mission to preach and teach a God in heaven who was a fully devoted follower of you?

Stop and think for a moment.

What if, in the grand scheme of salvation, it is God's intention to follow you immeasurably more than you ever followed him? What if God is infinitely more committed to you than you will ever be to him, *and he's good with that!?*

Let's break it down one more time.

Fully. One look at Calvary erases any questions about the extent of God's devotion to you. He is one hundred percent, completely, and without reservation "all in" for you.

Devoted. God is dedicated to you to the point of total sacrifice – with a "crazy love" so deep the human mind cannot fathom it.

Follower. He has been pursuing you all your days. He still is. If you really want the theme of "following" in the Christian life, here you go: "Surely goodness and mercy [grace] shall follow me [pursue me] All the days of my life; And I will dwell in the house of the Lord Forever" (Psalm 23:6). God is chasing you with his grace—that's what the Hebrew verb indicates. It's much stronger than mere following. God pursues you. Stop running like a maniac and let him catch you. That's the idea.

God is your fully devoted follower.

Breathe it in. Soak in that. Rest in that.

Let's make that astounding truth our ecclesiastical centerpiece. Let's make that our message. Our organizing principle. Let's make proclaiming that reality our mission.

"I am here today to declare to you that God is a fully devoted follower of you, and will be till you die."

If you run from him, he'll chase you with love. If you hide from him, he'll find you. If you cover your eyes, he'll patiently wait till you're ready to take a peek. "Whither shall I run from thy Spirit?" Nowhere. God is your fully devoted follower, and will be till the mountains crumble into the sea.

> - I AM HERE TODAY TO DECLARE TO YOU THAT GOD IS A FULLY DEVOTED FOLLOWER OF YOU, AND WILL BE TILL YOU DIE.

That will wake up the congregation.

It is impossible to make the centerpiece of the Christian message the arduous task of making people into fully devoted followers of Christ without first convincing them down to their toes that God is a fully devoted follower of them.

Grace first.

Grace next.

Grace responded to last.

ALL THE PROOF YOU NEED

Aside from the problem of swamping evangelism in a call for behavioral life-change, my other problem with *discipleship* as a concept is that it is too often viewed as an external, demonstrable, "proof" of salvation.

But is not the promise of God all the proof we need? If my Bible promises that whoever believes in Jesus will not perish, but will have everlasting life, and if I have believed in Jesus, isn't God's Word proof enough?

Discipleship has become code for *obedience*. It all-too-often bypasses the free-grace gospel, omits the saving work of Christ, neglects Calvary and the power of the shed blood, and is hyperfocused on behavior.

Above all else, discipleship is rarely rooted in an a systematic view of either sanctification or of grace.

In truth, the process of becoming a disciple is called *salvation*, and the process of making disciples is called *evangelism*.

The process of becoming a *good* disciple — a mature child of God — is called *sanctification* and the process of making good disciples is called *edification*. These biblical terms give us the clarity we need.

Correct terminology is foundational to correct thinking. It clears out the chaos.

We need a return to the old operating system that churches used for decades, one that separates what has always been separate: finding God (evangelism, salvation) and following God (edification, sanctification).

Finding God as Savior in salvation first.

Then following God as Lord, progressively, in sanctification, second.

Out of worry that people might fake their salvation, the church has essentially pressured Christians to fake their sanctification.

Nicely played, Mr. Devil.

ANDY STANLEY IS one of the most influential evangelical preachers in America today. In fact, a 2010 survey found him to be one of America's top ten most influential preachers. I imagine he's only grown in popularity since then. The son of Charles Stanley, his roots sink deeply into fundamentalist soil. So it created quite a stir when he told us all it was time to "unhitch our faith from the Old Testament" in his now infamous sermon, timed to coincide with the release of his 2019 book, *Irresistible.*

Think of what it means for a major evangelical leader to jettison three-quarters of the Bible.

The Bible!

Michael J. Kruger's analysis is exactly right: "According to Stanley, virtually everyone in the history of the church has been wrong about the role of the Old Testament—until now. It's truly a jaw-dropping claim."[1] Kruger is the president of Reformed Theological Seminary's Charlotte campus.

A "jaw-dropping claim" sums it up nicely.

And the fact that not enough jaws have dropped to at least reconsider his evangelical credentials proves my thesis of theological chaos pandemic in the church.

Someone might say, "You're taking Andy Stanley out of

context." I'm not. He says, "The Ten Commandments have no authority over you. None. To be clear: Thou shalt not obey the Ten Commandments" (136).

Again, Stanley's defenders might say, "You're not representing his position correctly." But he declares, "Paul never leverages the old covenant as a basis for Christian behavior" (209).

I read this and scratch my head, because, when I read Paul I find his whole argumentation a leveraging of Old Testament Scriptures to preach a Both Testaments faith:

> Owe no one anything except to love one another, for he who loves another has fulfilled the law. For the commandments, "You shall not commit adultery," "You shall not murder," "You shall not steal," "You shall not bear false witness," "You shall not covet," and if there is any other commandment, are all summed up in this saying, namely, "You shall love your neighbor as yourself." Love does no harm to a neighbor; therefore love is the fulfillment of the law. (Romans 13:8-10)

I'd call that whole Pauline paragraph a leveraging of the old covenant for Christian behavior. Stanley's assertions are flat out unbiblical.

Christians are already flaky enough with their Bibles. No Christian leader should ever utter a syllable that weakens our trust in and stance upon the sixty-six books of Scripture.

> - NO CHRISTIAN LEADER SHOULD EVER UTTER A
> SYLLABLE THAT WEAKENS OUR TRUST IN AND STANCE
> UPON THE SIXTY-SIX BOOKS OF SCRIPTURE.

Why does Andy Stanley go here? He says it is for the sake of evangelism. I'm all for evangelism, so.... fine. He suggests, in a nutshell, that the reason we Christians are losing the younger generation is the offensiveness of Old Testament stories and laws. Therefore, to make the gospel message "irresistible," we must "unhitch our faith from the Old Testament."

Not fine.

Welcome to a church ruled by people who are better leaders and more engaging speakers than they are expositors of Scripture.

THE WHOLE BIBLE FOR THE WHOLE CHURCH

Stanley's confusion is on full display when he writes,

> The fact that someone chose to publish the old covenant with the new covenant in a genuine leather binding doesn't mean we should treat them or apply them the same way. The Bible is all God's Word . . . to somebody. But it's not all God's word to everybody.[2]

Do not misunderstand what he is saying. He is arguing that the first 39 books of the Sacred canon should no longer be included within the genuine leather covers of our Bibles. In his words, they are not "God's word" to us, the church, the people of God today.

This able exposition of the ancient Marcionite heresy must not go unchallenged. Justin Martyr (AD 110-165), Irenaeus (AD 130-200), and Hippolytus (AD 170-235) nailed Marcion of Sinope to the wall for it in the second century, and it's time to do the same to Andy Stanley in the run up to the twenty-second century.

He flat out *admits* he's flirting with the charge of heresy: "I'm not suggesting the two testaments are not equally inspired. My point is they aren't equally applicable. As heretical as that may sound, consider this..."[3] Stanley proceeds to argue that readers of John and other New Testament books have gotten saved by reading them, but this doesn't happen with Old Testament books. See? Time to unhitch.

Application follows after interpretation. If you do your

interpretation right, *every* portion of Scripture is equally applicable to the people of God in every age.

The testimony of both Scripture and history is that all of the Bible is the book of God. All the Bible is the book of Grace. All the Bible is relevant for all the people of God of all ages. To say that there are differentiations in application is one thing—evangelical scholars agree. But to say we should unhitch our faith is another thing altogether.

The fact that Andy Stanley cannot find the grace he's looking for in the Old Testament says more about his theological blinders than about the Scriptures.

Having grown up in a dispensational theology, I understand his position deep down in my bones. But Stanley goes beyond dispensationalism to ultra-dispensationalism, something the late, great Harry Ironside — himself a dispensationalist — called "wrongly dividing the word of truth."[4]

A COVENANT DOES NOT A TESTAMENT MAKE

Andy Stanley erroneously conflates the Old Covenant with the Old Testament. He says, "Bottom line: 'covenant' and 'testament' are interchangeable."[5]

Not so fast.

The Old *Testament* is the body of 39 books.

The Old *Covenant* is a teaching within those books. The Old Covenant teaching emphasizes divine law and divine wrath for those who fall short. It then reveals divine grace as the generous gift bequeathed by God. It specifies the conditions under which humans qualify to participate as heirs of God. It shows how God, through the death of the Savior to come, unlocked the vaults of heaven, bequeathing an inheritance and eternal life to all who would join the tribe of believing Abraham.

J. Barton Payne's, *A Theology of the Older Testament*, is a groundbreaking work in this regard. I wish Stanley had steeped his mind in such teaching before he announced his unfortunate conclusions.

Contrary to popular belief, within the books of the Old Testament itself, the Old Covenant of Works is displaced by the New Testament of Grace.

Paul himself said so:

> And this I say, that the law, which was four hundred and thirty years later, cannot annul the [testament] that was confirmed before by God in Christ, that it should make the promise of no effect. For if the inheritance is of the law, it is no longer of promise; but God gave it to Abraham by promise. (Galatians 3:17, 18)

In other words, the Old Testament itself, teaches a movement from a covenant of works (Edenic) to a covenant of grace (Abrahamic).

As if that's not enough, it teaches it again in the movement from a covenant of law (Mosaic), back to a covenant of grace (Davidic, called the *new/renewed* covenant by Jeremiah, which is really the Abarahamic covenant all over again).

The exact same movement happens in the New Testament (Hebrews 8:6). In other words, all of Scripture is God's heavenly shout to startle us from works to grace, from salvation by earning it to salvation by inheriting it as the last will and testament of a Crucified and Risen Savior.

Old Testament scholar, Walter Kaiser, once quipped, "I love the New Testament—it reminds me so much of the Old."[6]

"God is love" is written in the New Testament, but it is only there as the summation of a million echoes and whispers from the Old Testament. The God revealed in the Law and the Prophets is one who nurses his children like a loving mother, and gathers us under his wings like a hen gathers her chicks. He is tender-hearted and abundant in *hesed* (grace).

That's *how* John came to know that God is love, and that's *why* he came to write it. He read his Bible.

In reply to all this, D.A. Carson succinctly states, "We need Jesus, so we need the Old Testament."[7]

We need a healthy dose of Vitamin OT to grow strong spiritual bones and bulging evangelistic muscles.

YOU SHOULD HAVE KNOWN

The Old Testament can stand on its own. It teaches and presents the New Covenant in great, though not complete, fulness. Why else would Jesus rebuke the disciples on the road to Emmaus for what he considered culpable ignorance?

> Then He said to them, "O foolish ones, and slow of heart to believe in all that the prophets have spoken! Ought not the Christ to have suffered these things and to enter into His glory?" And beginning at Moses and all the Prophets, He expounded to them in all the Scriptures the things concerning Himself. (Luke 24:25-27)

Wouldn't Jesus confront Andy Stanley with the same rebuke today? "Foolish," Jesus said. "Slow of heart to believe." From his perspective, the Old Testament books revealed the New Testament promises in enough detail to render people responsible to understand and believe.

Like generations before us, we must insist: Do not mess with the Bible.

Do not add to it.

Do not subtract from it.

Interpret it. That's your job.

If we cannot agree on what constitutes our Bible, how can we agree on anything? Is this not the starting place for all theology? For all truth?

Is not any position that discounts "resistible" portions of Scripture the starting point for heresy?

Stanley has since tried to walk this back, but his original statements are clear and his walk-backs are far too little.[8]

The damage is done.

Am I being divisive? All truth is divisive. It cannot be otherwise. The purpose of a doctrinal statement is to define us, and, therefore, to differentiate us from those who hold incompatible positions. We can do this in love, but we cannot do it without pointing out where our paths diverge.

If Stanley had said we should jettison James, or Mark, or Revelation, he would have been shown the evangelical door, and rightly so.

What is wrong with us that we can still listen to him having discarded 39 books of the inspired text? And make no mistake, this is exactly what he affirms.

Besides, if broadening our evangelistic reach is the goal, why stop with the Old Testament? Following Stanley's logic, shouldn't we cut out the offensive parts of Romans — especially where Paul talks about the wrath of God and sexual sins? And what about the teachings on hell by Jesus and in the book of Revelation? While we're at it, James is pretty heavy, so let's cut that out too.

Pretty soon, all we're left with is Jefferson's Bible with all the offensive bits cut out.

God help us the day we start letting soft heresy in the door.

ALL YOU NEED IS THE RESURRECTION?

Stanley builds a case that the whole church is built strictly on the historical event of the Resurrection of Jesus.

As he puts it, "Resurrection is the horse. The Bible is the cart."[9]

He goes so far as to say, "Your whole house of Old Testament cards can come tumbling down. The question is did Jesus rise from the dead?" Michael Brown called this, "a staggeringly dangerous claim."[10]

There are two fatal flaws in Stanley's line of argumentation. One is the hyperbolic emphasis on the resurrection. The second is the divorce between the events of Scripture and the words of Scripture.

The early church indeed majored in the resurrection. Every sermon in Acts mentions it. But Stanley disfigures Christianity when he, a) elevates the event beyond biblical proportions, and b) separates the event itself from the written text.

What are we supposed to say? "Hey, I have good news! Jesus rose from the dead!" Then what do we say? How do we make the case? How do we summon our eyewitnesses without quoting our Bibles? How do we explain its meaning and its promise and its hope if the resurrection event is quarantined from the resurrection Scriptures?

Stanley makes the resurrection the only thing that matters:

> So yes, there once existed a version of our faith that rested securely on a single unprecedented event—the resurrection. That's the version I'm inviting you to embrace. The original version. The endurable, defensible, new covenant, new command version. (321, 322)

But what about the single unprecedented event of, say, the death of Christ? Wasn't this the apostolic Prime Directive?

- For I determined not to know anything among you except Jesus Christ and Him crucified. (1 Corinthians 2:2)
- But God forbid that I should boast except in the cross of our Lord Jesus Christ, by whom the world has been crucified to me, and I to the world. (Galatians 6:14)
- But we preach Christ crucified, to the Jews a stumbling block and to the Greeks foolishness, (1 Corinthians 1:23)

Is not the death of Christ of at least equal importance to the resurrection? After all, the Lord's Supper was instituted to "proclaim the Lord's death," not his resurrection, "till he comes" (1 Corinthians 11:26). That's the main thing.

So why isn't the Cross of Christ Stanley's "single unprecedented event"? Or why not the second coming? Or the gift of salvation? Or the incarnation?

It's a mess.

But the mess is compounded by Stanley's insistence that the singular event of the resurrection be *divorced from the scriptural texts that reveal it and give it meaning.*

Proclaim the resurrection, but not the Bible. That's his point. For real.

The whole approach displays a painful imbalance on numerous levels.

The apostles explicitly devoted themselves to the texts of the Word of God—which, in their day, meant the Old Testament—and to prayer.

Stanley's position is historically indefensible. His argument runs counter to the facts. Even worse, he utterly neglects that the Resurrection of Jesus is the divine exclamation point on the Crucifixion of Jesus and all that it means.

Tell me for heaven's sake how "the Lamb of God taking away the sin of the world" makes any sense at all without a thorough knowledge of its antecedents, all of which are in the Old Testament. Do you want to really appreciate what Jesus did on Calvary? Study the five kinds of sacrifices described in Leviticus. You just might shout *Hallelujah!*

Furthermore, Stanley's position denies the power of proclaiming God's Word.

Stanley actually marshalls a case for his advice that — wait for it — preachers and evangelists and Christians everywhere should quit saying, "The Bible says..."

Again, the problem with *the Bible says* is what else the Bible says. If you preach, teach, write curriculum, lead a small group, or talk about your faith in public, drop the phrases *the Bible says* and *the Bible teaches*. There's nothing to be gained. There's much to be lost. As in our credibility and the next generation.[11]

Raise your hand if your jaw just dropped.

Is this not disturbing?

Is this not cheap epistemology on steroids?

He goes on to make the case for an erroneous and discredited teaching called neo-orthodoxy, concluding, "Again, the foundation of our faith is not an inspired book but the events that inspired the book."[12]

Wait a minute. It was *events* that inspired God's Book? Oh. And all this time I was thinking it was the Holy Spirit.

Andy Stanley is asking us not only to unhitch our faith from the Old Testament, but to actually unhitch our proclamation from the Bible.

Alarm!

Send help!

Wake up!

We were so taken aback by the call to unhitch from the Old Testament, that we missed the call to unhitch from both testaments.

THE B.I.B.L.E. ONCE AGAIN

What built the early church was the dynamic power of the Word of God, starting with the Old Testament alone, and by accretion, growing into the New Testament too. What built the early church was "the foolishness of preaching."

For Paul, the word "Scripture" was an explicit reference to the Old Testament canon:

> All Scripture is given by inspiration of God, and is profitable for doctrine, for reproof, for correction, for instruction in righteousness, that the man of God may be complete, thoroughly equipped for every good work. (2 Timothy 3:16, 17)

Can the Old Testament's profitability for today's church be any clearer?

Peter told us to "heed" the "prophetic word," not to unhitch from it (2 Peter 1:19).

The Author of Hebrews tells us "the Word of God is living and powerful" (4:12).

Paul told Timothy to "preach the Word" (2 Timothy 4:2).

The Word was the weapon Jesus wielded against Satan, and it remains the Spirit's sword against demons today.

Far from pushing Gentiles away from the gospel, as Stanley suggests, it was the teaching of the Old Testament that caused them to beg for more: "So when the Jews went out of the synagogue, the Gentiles begged that these words might be preached to them the next Sabbath" (Acts 13:42).

Paul said he was "not ashamed of the gospel of Christ, for it is the power of God unto salvation to all who believe" (Romans 1:18).

"Thus saith the Lord" remains the mightiest weapon in the church's world-changing arsenal. To say otherwise is a mistake of epic proportions.

My point is less about Andy Stanley, and more about a church-at-large that yawns at such erroneous teaching. Don't get me wrong. He is a gifted leader. He is a phenomenal communicator. He seems like a very nice, fun, and funny guy. God loves him and so do I, despite our disagreements.

I applaud Stanley's passion for evangelism. I love the idea of removing roadblocks to salvation. What I cannot applaud is building a safe-zone around the gospel that won't let the Bible in.

I cannot wrap my mind around a gospel message that is actually ashamed of the Bible.

Astonishing.

J. Barton Payne — one of those evangelical giants of yesteryear so sorely missed by today's church — declared,

Many people today fail to appreciate the relevance of the theology of the older testament. Actually, however, its truths contain the permanent solutions to the greatest questions of human life, for "the grass withereth, the flower fadeth; but the word of our God shall stand forever" (Isa. 40:8).[13]

There are two teams here.

J. Barton Payne and a likeminded tribe of theological heavyweights who find in the Old Testament "the permanent solutions to the greatest questions of human life."

Or...

Andy Stanley and a likeminded tribe of theological pragmatists who find in the Old Testament only irritations to the modern mind which must therefore be summarily dismissed.

Choose your team wisely.

As for me and my house, we will stand with the Savior who said, "O my God... your Law is within my heart" (Psalm 40:8).

ONE LAST THING

One last thing.

Who made it the church's job to make the gospel "irresistible?" The message of salvation through Christ crucified and risen again is, was, and always will be a stumbling block, a *skandalon*.

It is exclusive — Jesus is the only way.

It is offensive — you are a helpless, hopeless sinner, and you need a Savior.

It is pure charity — you are such a wreck that it cost the Son of God his blood to save your sorry soul.

You simply cannot erase the offense.

The only way to make the Christian message "irresistible" is to erase Christ, the Great Divider. And the only way to do that is to toss out Scripture.

Let us pray that day never comes.

Above all else, to call into question the authority of any part of Scripture is to wreak epistemological havoc on the church, and to unleash even more chaos into the divine sheepfold. The Bible on which we stand contains sixty-six canonical, divinely authoritative, perfectly harmonious books. Let us pray future generations of the church will take their stand on this same inerrant Word.

---

1. Michael J. Kruger, "Why We Can't Unhitch from the Old Testament" from the Gospel Coalition, retrieved June 19, 2020 from https://www. thegospelcoalition.org/reviews/irresistible-andy-stanley/.
2. Ibid. 99.
3. Stanley, Andy. *Irresistible* (p. 103). Zondervan. Kindle Edition.
4. Ironside was the popular pastor of Chicago's historic Moody Church. You can find his booklet in the public domain here: https://www. wholesomewords.org/etexts/ironside/wrongly.pdf
5. Stanley, Andy. *Irresistible* (p. 97). Zondervan. Kindle Edition.
6. From a personal conversation reported at https://www.michaelrydelnik. org/hitched-old-testament/ and relieved, June 28, 2020.
7. In the Gospel Coalition podcast for December 18, 2018 retrieved June 19, 2020 from https://www.thegospelcoalition.org/podcasts/tgc-podcast/ need-jesus-need-old-testament/.
8. "Andy Stanley Responds to Criticism About His 'Unhitching' From the Old Testament Sermon, in *Relevant*, July 5, 2018. At https:// relevantmagazine.com/god/andy-stanley-explains-why-hes-stopped-saying-the-bible-says/, retrieved April 16, 2019.
9. Stanley, Andy. *Irresistible* (p. 299). Zondervan. Kindle Edition.
10. From https://askdrbrown.org/library/no-pastor-stanley-we-should-not-unhitch-ourselves-old-testament retrieved June 28, 2020.
11. Stanley, Andy. *Irresistible* (p. 307). Zondervan. Kindle Edition.
12. Stanley, Andy. *Irresistible* (p. 315). Zondervan. Kindle Edition.
13. J. Barton Payne, *The Theology of the Older Testament*, Zondervan, 1962, iii.

A QUICK AND unscientific survey of pastor-search websites shows an inescapable conclusion: above all else, churches demand "visionary leaders" in their pastorates. All the other stuff is there, to be sure. But "visionary leader" takes center stage.

What does this *mean*?

I first met John Maxwell during my doctoral program. He lectured for about eight hours, and called me Gio-spaghetti. I actually felt special. At the time, he was pastoring in southern California. He would go on to become a preeminent expert in leadership, and write about three thousand books on the topic. Pastors snapped them up, and rightly so. Dr. Maxwell eventually left the pastorate to teach leaders to lead, both inside and outside of the church.

I consider that a demotion. Yes, he followed God's call on his life (presumably). And yes, God has multiplied his ministry beyond measure. But hear me out.

To paraphrase Martyn Lloyd-Jones, preaching is the most glorious calling to which a person can aspire. There is nothing higher, and no calling more important. Preaching is the most important activity of the church. Only the preacher's preparation for the task of preaching comes in second place. As Paul said, "I magnify my ministry" (Romans 11:13). I love John Maxwell, but the day he left the pulpit, he took a step away from the most glorious call God can give a human being.

Leadership, even visionary leadership, represents a step down from the glorious ministry of preaching.

I'll trade you one good Bible teacher for a thousand visionary leaders. I would rather sit under a faithful preacher who delivered the goods of Scripture than under a visionary leader any day. The leader's incessant visionary trumpet-blast will wear me out. At least a faithful preacher, plodding along verse-by-verse, will serve up fodder for my weary soul. The faithful preacher will edify me and equip me for life and mission. The faithful preacher will remind me of transcendent realities that bear upon my every day life and give meaning to the mundane.

Professors attend conferences on theology and evangelicalism.

Pastors attend conferences on leadership.

Isn't this a little sideways and a whole lot backwards?

WHO STOLE OUR THEOLOGY?

I have paid good money to attend those leadership gatherings. They are largely excellent and extremely fun. I can tell you, however, firsthand, what we never talk about: theology. It just doesn't come up. We're not there for theological conversation anyway. We're there to become better *leaders*, so we can lead more people into so-called encounters with God where truth is less relevant than the encounter.

The irony stings my throat.

A second-rate preacher can never be a first-rate leader. This is because, for the Church, preaching *is* leading. When the apostles handed off day to day leadership to the deacons/administrators, they reserved for themselves the single most influential aspect of leadership through the ministry of the Word. Preaching was their main calling, and their central authority, and their functional leadership all wrapped together. To set leading over preaching is to damage both. But, when we celebrate the primacy of preaching, the church looks to the pulpit for leadership, and finds it there in the most natural and spiritually satisfying way possible.

The primacy of preaching necessitates the primacy of study. Paul, while in prison, urged Timothy to "bring... the books" (2 Timothy 4:13). A student of Scripture till the bitter end. Has the church ever benefitted from a better leader? If the preachers are to lead well, they must plant their butts in the chair, shut the door, and study long and hard. While the saints are out doing the work of the ministry, the pastor must break a sweat mining the ore of Scripture, refining the gold, and preparing to deliver it in the ONE work that makes all the other works possible (Ephesians 4:12).

Dear Pastor, please study deep and hard, because neither charisma nor leadership techniques can ever compensate for laziness in pulpit preparation.

What does the text say? What do the words mean? What does this partictular genitive construct mean in this particular passage? Why did James say it this way and not that way? How does Esther follow Moses, and how does Ruth further the line of the Messiah? Where's the grace in the text? How is this not contradicting that?

Unless pastors wrestle with the Word, the people won't be edified enough to wrestle with the world.

- UNLESS PASTORS WRESTLE WITH THE WORD, THE PEOPLE WON'T BE EDIFIED ENOUGH TO WRESTLE WITH THE WORLD.

So please, Pastor, for the love of your church, turn your back on us and turn your face to God in his Word, and bolt the door shut behind you so nobody interrupts.

Even Jesus carved out large swaths of time for solitude.

An hour in the study for every minute in the pulpit.

Anything less leaves untouched the chaos in our thinking and therefore in our lives.

But this brings us back to "visionary leadership" and what might be its most subtle malignancy of all.

EXTROVERSION

In too many cases, visionary leadership has become code for extroversion. Pastor search committees seek pastors with huge relational capacity so they can know and love the flock — every last member. They want to be inspired. They want to be fired up. They want a pep rally to grow the church, and to love the people.

All of this is well and good, but it requires an extroverted pastor. And the extroverted pastor is exactly the person who dreads the solitary confinement of a closed office door and a musty stack of books.

It is counterintuitive, but introverted pastors are disproportionately represented among large church pastors. This is because introverts are drawn to the solitary confinement and the bookish ideation needed to produce startlingly meaningful expositions of Scripture, which in turn fuel the church's mission. But most churches resent the "unavailable" pastor. Unless pastors spend the bulk of their days in public, politicking and ministering and serving tables, the givers, I mean the people, might not feel they're getting their money's worth.

So "Give us a visionary leader!" they say, "and a people-person who is highly relational." And with that the church has demanded an extrovert, thereby unwittingly setting a ceiling on the spiritual growth of its people and on the evangelistic potential of its mission.

It is clear that God uses introverts and extroverts alike. It is also clear he is able to use a visionary leader too, in equal measure as the jawbone of an ass. God is God. But whatever crisis exists in the church cannot be solved by elevating theologically shallow leaders to the pastorate, no matter how visionary or appealing they may be.

God help us.

We have stimulated an appetite for the wrong thing. It's not leadership we need, per se. It's the depths of the wonders of God and the heights of the grandeur of redemption and the breadth of the Spirit's sanctification that will deliver us from our chaotic malaise. May our pulpits revel in that.

Now *that's* a vision I can get behind.

It is the hard-working biblical expositor who is essential.

Visionary leadership is optional.

I EMBRACE A THEOLOGICAL PERSPECTIVE some have labeled
the Free Grace Movement. I am happy with that label, because
what's not to like? It's free. It's grace. No, I don't endorse everything the Free Grace Movement stands for, but I'm sure the
feeling is mutual. That's where charity comes in.

I also feel certain affinities toward what is called Sovereign
Grace, a euphemism for Calvinism, though my theological
disagreements there are more pronounced.

As a guy who's known for a grace-oriented theology, I am
routinely greeted with enthusiastic statements such as, "My
pastor preaches grace too!" Or, "We have a new song about
grace." Or, "I'm glad God is gracious, because I'm such a
wreck." The people I meet in my travels are generally eager to
show that their church/ministry/book/etc. proclaims grace too.

Nevertheless, the simple fact of the matter is that the evangelical church has unceremoniously murdered grace. We have
committed this crime by misuse, dilution, and the death of a
thousand cuts.

The great Bible teacher and founder of Dallas Theological
Seminary, Lewis Sperry Chafer, began his book on grace by
saying, "The precise and discriminate meaning of the word
grace ought to be crystal clear to every child of God."

Now, there's an "ought" I can get behind.

The problem is that we are not "crystal clear," not even close. We barely reach the "murky" threshold. The church is to blame. The church at large has murdered grace, thereby relegating the people of God to the terminally stunted Phariseeism which Jesus verbally crucified.

Once again, the motive for this crime is less obvious than it might at first appear. Let's dispatch a few obvious motives, and then get down to brass knuckles.

THE OBVIOUS STUFF

We can rattle off quite a few obvious reasons for the death of grace in the church today. We have already fretted over a general theological illiteracy in the land, which easily applies to the rigorous doctrine we call grace. We have also lamented the thug ironically called ultra-tolerance, and the way it has bullied itself into churches and seminaries today. Unless we're virtue-signaling our acceptance — actually *advocacy* —of every moral deviancy that has a name, we're accused of being anti-grace.

Perhaps a deeper etching on Grace's tombstone says something as simple as *They Never Understood the Cross*. And it's true. By neglecting theology, we have starved God's children of the meat of Calvary: propitiation, expiation, regeneration, redemption, vicarious substitution, and all the doctrines stained crimson by Jesus' blood.

The heart of Scripture is Christ. The heart of Christ is grace. The heart of Grace is the Cross.

Without Christ's Cross, there is no grace, not in reality, and not conceptually either. There is no such thing as a Christless grace, yet this is certainly abroad in the land. But even worse, there is no such thing as a Crossless grace, and this is pandemic.

Every time we say that God accepts you just as you are, we think we are talking about grace, when in reality we are jabbing a knife in grace's back *unless we connect that acceptance to the Old Rugged Cross.*

Every time we tell an immoral person not to worry because God forgives them, we only set them up for an even deeper guilt later on, unless we explain exactly how and where that forgiveness was procured. We need a forgiveness that means something — one that the devil can't undermine — and such a forgiveness requires ideational linkages to the Cross.

The late, great Australian New Testament scholar, Leon Morris, did the English-speaking church a massive favor when he wrote two books specifically on the cross. In 1955, he penned *The Apostolic Preaching of the Cross*. In this marvelous book, he delves into the precise meanings of the words I have already lamented for dropping out of the Christian vocabulary: justification, propitiation, etc. In each chapter, he traces the apostolic preaching as rooted in the Old Testament and wending its way through the New, and then into the early church. He lapses into Greek and Hebrew with liberality and writes for the studious pastor or seminary student. I re-read this book every other year, and find new wonders in it every time. Morris shows what it meant for Peter, Paul, John, and all the apostles to preach the Cross of Christ.

If this isn't the foundation of grace, nothing is.

I used to assign this book in my seminary classes.

I can no longer do so, as so many no longer take Greek and Hebrew.

No worries, however, as Morris put out a more accessible version of the same book in 1983 called *The Atonement*. He covers the same ground at a less technical level.

Back to the main point. I am saying that the church has murdered grace, and one of the stab wounds is our fundamental ignorance of the most important thing of all: the meaning of the Cross of Christ. Oh, we have some idea of it, but it's not enough to silence the devil. Perhaps even worse, it is not enough to answer faith-destroying critics who would turn the vicarious death of Christ into a mere moral example or something less. It takes a scholar to silence a scholar, and the evangelical church's scholars are dying off faster than they're being replaced.

To divorce grace from the Cross is to murder it. In most places, the corpse has already stopped twitching. Grace has devolved into a general synonym for *nice*, or *lenient*, or something God-awfully wimpy like that. That's why we can sing *Amazing Grace* at an unsaved drug-dealer's funeral, and assume that God is nice enough not to damn anybody. What else would you expect from a bunch of theologically stunted spiritual brats?

Crossless grace is an abomination that meshes perfectly with our post-modern, deconstructed, intersectionalized preference for subjectivity over truth.

But this divide from Calvary's Cross, as bad as it is, is not the real perp in Grace's tragic murder. No. The real murderer is more insidious and harder to spot.

How, exactly, did the church murder grace?

WHEN WE START IN THE MIDDLE

In Romans 8:1, Paul declares the wonderful truth that every grace-preacher rightly loves to shout from the rooftops:

> There is therefore now no condemnation for those who are in Christ Jesus. (Romans 8:1, NASB)

How amazing! No condemnation. None. Zero. Gone. Such grace! The most beautiful, liberating, counter-intuitive words the world has ever heard. The dying world around us is starving for this victorious proclamation.

So is the church.

Yes, we've heard it a million times. Any self-respecting Christian already knows it. *God doesn't condemn me. There is no condemnation for me.* Everybody knows it, because, well, grace!

Yet, the devil still has a field day with us. We still don't get it. The enormity of the grace packed into Romans 8:1 has simply not settled in deeply enough among Christians.

Why not?

Because we started at Romans 8:1, that's why not. We jumped to the middle.

You can come to me as your pastor, loaded with guilt and shame over something you said to your kid. I can turn to Romans 8:1 and comfort you. "God doesn't condemn you. You don't need to live with that shame. You can move beyond that guilt." All of that is true and correct. It is also genuinely helpful — at least for a day or two.

But, haven't we forgotten something?

Haven't we forgotten Romans 1:1 through Romans 7:25? Unless I consistently backfill the argument for you, the conclusion has no staying power.

Romans 8:1 wasn't written in a vacuum. My Sunday School teachers taught me a simple yet profound lesson: when you see the word *therefore*, stop and ask what it's *there for*. In this case, it's there to introduce a conclusion. The conclusion flows from the tightly reasoned logic of the seven preceding chapters. Like a brilliant lawyer, Paul patiently constructs his case. He builds his argument, truth by truth, ascending in thought and wonder, till he reaches the epic conclusion of Romans 8:1 and all that follows.

To skip all that is to murder grace. There's the real culprit. Starting in the middle. That's how the church murdered grace.

Christian teachers do with grace what Oprah famously did with new cars. You get a new car! You get a new car! You get a new car! And you get a new car too! Grace for all. You get grace! And you get grace! And you get grace too!

This feel-good moment has been brought to you, presumably, by grace.

Only it isn't grace. Today's grace is a conclusion without an argument, and is therefore only as strong as a house without a foundation. To put it another way, grace relates to the doctrines of God, sin, depravity, Christology, and soteriology in the same way that a rose relates to its roots. Can you enjoy the rose without its roots? Yes. But you can't keep a rose without the roots for very long, and the church let the roots dry out a long time ago.

So we hand out plastic imitations of the real thing.

The approach ought to be different. Profoundly, radically, annoyingly different. In the same breath with which we teach the grace of "no condemnation," we should also be teaching the case for no condemnation. Bit by bit. Line by line.

> - IN THE SAME BREATH WITH WHICH WE TEACH THE GRACE OF "NO CONDEMNATION," WE SHOULD ALSO BE TEACHING THE CASE FOR NO CONDEMNATION.

Grace is a doctrinal palace. Let's roll up our sleeves and build it. Because if we don't, we only build a house of cards, an apt description for much of American Christianity.

We are busy handing out feel-good coffee cards, when we should be building theological edifices.

We hand out a grace that looks and smells like leniency, when Scripture is clear that God is anything but lenient.

We neuter grace into a bland niceness, and have effectively clipped the claws of the Lion of the Tribe of Judah.

We rush grace into the picture long before the Law has finished its work of slaying self-sufficiency and pride. No sin, no guilt. No guilt, no fear. No fear, no grace.

While Scripture paints a portrait of sinners *fleeing for refuge* to lay hold of their only hope in Christ, we muzzle the Hound of Heaven, chain him in the back yard, and deprive sinners of any frightful prospect that might motivate them to flee. Today's insipid gospel invites unregenerate people on a journey to nowhere, as if they're actually able to lift a foot.

God help us.

We have let grace slip into the realm of tolerance. We have wiped from the church's memory the crimson cross as an emblem of the blistering intolerance of our holy God.

A word is a placeholder for an idea. When we use a word, we hope it conjures in the mind of our audience the same idea it conjured in ours. What is conjured in your mind when you hear the word *grace*? Is it blood-bought? Is it Christ Centered and Cross Centered? Is it the hard, tough, exacting, rigorous, compelling conclusion from a complex edifice of doctrine?

If not, we've murdered it. The church has made grace into baby food. We've skipped the first seven chapters to find "The End" and called it good.

GOD'S LOVE DIED TOO

We have done the same thing with God's love. If I hear one more ditzy Christian declare that God's love is *unconditional*, I'm going to stick my finger down my throat and barf on their shoes. On purpose.

God's love is exceedingly conditional — at least our experience of it is. God's love is conditioned on the substitutionary death of Christ. God's love *in our experience* is conditioned on membership in the family of faith. Our ongoing *experience* of God's love is conditioned upon our ongoing faith in the one who "loved us and gave his life for us" (Galatians 2:20).

For those who do not know Christ, God's love exists in a general way under the concept of common grace. But the primary way God relates to an unsaved person is not love but divine justice. They are under condemnation already. "The wrath of God abides on them." They relate to God only as Judge, because they have not fled to him as Savior, so they do not get to call him Abba.

God's love is extremely conditional, so let's put that little cliché to rest.

The good news is that in grace, God has fulfilled all the conditions—those requiring moral performance—by his own power and work. *He* did that. It is finished. It is finished by God himself. The performance-based conditions have all been fulfilled, so now God's love can flow. The only condition that's left is the un-performance called faith, which fixes us under the umbrella of previously-met-conditions forever.

But to forget those conditions — fulfilled in and by Christ "and him crucified" alone — is to murder grace and love, and that is the point I've been trying to make all along.

If you skip straight to Romans 8:1, the grace of "no condemnation" is neutered. If you skip right to being "accepted" in the Beloved One, without teaching what it means to be "in the Beloved One," the acceptance turns out to be candy without nutrition. If you fail to unpack the blood of Christ, the forgiveness tied to that blood in Ephesians 1:7 loses its staying power. Instead, we tell people God accepts them, and God forgives them, and God doesn't condemn them in ways that don't even scratch the surface of grace.

And that's why, though grace might rise to the level of *interesting,* it almost never even comes close to *amazing.*

But it gets worse.

ENTITLED

When we skip the doctrines that undergird grace, not only do we murder grace, but we also create an entitlement mentality for the favors and blessings that flow from grace. Today's church *presumes* upon the grace of God. We clip along assuming that we're good with God when we're not. As a cat hacks up a fur ball, Jesus is righteously busy hacking us up to spew us out of his mouth, and we haven't got a clue.

I am not denying the genuineness of anyone's salvation. If you, knowing your sinfulness, have trusted Christ — and him crucified and risen again — you are saved. You have been born again, forgiven, and adopted into God's family. You are bound for heaven, and God's love and grace are lavished upon you. I affirm all that without reservation.

Even so I affirm you, or I, may very well be a clueless idiot, in Christian love. The lukewarm church of Laodicea was adjudged lukewarm for presuming everything was good as far as God was concerned while forgetting they were — apart from grace — "wretched, miserable, poor, blind, and naked"

(Revelation 3:17). We always are and always will be charity cases.

The moment you forget you are a charity case is the moment you feel entitled to good stuff from your wealthy Heavenly Grandfather, and this is the moment you murder grace. *I can do this sin, God will forgive me. I can express this moral perversion, God loves me, and I'm special. I'm God's favorite. I can't lose, and I can't fail, because grace!*

In truth, your ungodly behavior as a child of God can never separate you from the *possession* of God's love and grace. It can, however, separate you from the *experience* of that love and grace, and this is the chronic condition of our chaotic church today. Your mere existence gives you no claim on the grace of God. Calvary does that, and if you don't enter by that door, forget about it.

The beginning of entitlement is the end of grace.

Murderers! Spiritually stunted spoiled brats, beloved of God nonetheless! Farewell, sweet Grace. R.I.P.

THANK GOD

Thank God for grace. I mean that literally, as an imperative. Every single day, thank God for a blood-bought, Satan-silencing, sin-crushing, life-energizing grace. The only thing we deserve from God is damnation. Thank God for the Cross. We are entitled to nothing, and yet given everything. Thank God for Jesus. We now walk in the realm of unfailing love. Thank God for the riches of our salvation.

Make the case for grace. Start at the beginning. Or, start in the middle and then backfill if you must. Follow Paul's argument leading up to Romans 8:1 and all of Scripture's other arguments too. I'm not saying that we all need Bible degrees to benefit from the conclusions of grace — I am just arguing that we all need to enroll in the *school* of grace and stay there. Otherwise, the experience of grace dies, and we have effectively murdered it.

Grace will rise from the dead when Christians return to the knowledge of the Cross and of the Savior who hung on it. And we can only return to the knowledge of the Cross and of Christ when we return to the deep things of the beautifully complex Scripture, for it is Scripture alone that unveils God's matchless grace in all its wondrous glory.

⸻

Beneath the Cross of Jesus I fain would take my stand,
The shadow of a mighty Rock within a weary land;
A home within the wilderness, a rest upon the way,
From the burning of the noon-tide heat and the burden of the day.

Upon the Cross of Jesus, mine eye at times can see
The very dying form of One who suffered there for me:
And from my stricken heart with tears, two wonders I confess,
The wonders of redeeming love, and my unworthiness.

I take, O Cross, thy shadow for my abiding place:
I ask no other sunshine than the sunshine of his face;
Content to let the world go by, to know no gain nor loss;
My sinful self my only shame, my glory all the cross.

– ELIZABETH CECELIA CLEPHANE, 1850

PARDON THE PLAY on a famous political line—"It's the economy, stupid"—but it's important to know that all of the disturbing trends we have seen are not disconnected bits floating on a sea of chaos. They are, rather, gnarly outgrowths from a single malignant root.

It's the devil, stupid.

The fact that the body of Christ has forgotten this, and scarcely references it with any theological accuracy, is my final disturbing trend in today's church. It is the ground and being of every other disturbing trend too.

Chaos is irrationality's excrement. And irrationality is the devil's calling card. Sin is irrational. A coup against heaven is irrational. A wolf dressed in sheep's clothing is irrational.

I am coming to realize that every time I scratch my head over something in the church or in the world and say, "That makes no sense whatsoever," the devil is only inches away, laughing in the corner.

It is too kind to say that irrationality is just uninformed, or stupid, or senseless. Irrationality is evil. It is, in fact, the essence of evil. It is the unreality of demonic lies battering themselves against the bedrock laws of our eternal God.

The lies of Satan will burn themselves out trying to beat up God's people. Herein lies the chaos. The Church, grounded in scriptural truth, will prevail—ultimately, in the long run.

The near term is another story.

MORE CUNNING

> Now the serpent was more cunning than any beast of the field which the LORD God had made. And he said to the woman, "Has God indeed said, 'You shall not eat of every tree of the garden'?" (Genesis 3:1)

When the Bible introduces us to Satan, the first description applied to him is "cunning." Different translations say subtle, crafty, shrewd, and wise.

Of all the possible descriptors of the devil, this is the one that is most easily forgotten. This dark lord is cunning. He is crafty. He is wily.

But this is forgotten. It is forgotten by pastors. It is forgotten by Christians. It is forgotten by politicians. It is forgotten by the world. It is forgotten by virtually every person posting on social media, including most Christians.

The Head and Fount of all evil, and murder, and darkness, and deception in the world is, above all else, *subtle*.

Much later, in the New Testament, St. Paul would say the same thing: "And no wonder! For Satan himself transforms himself into an angel of light" (2 Corinthians 11:14).

What does this cunning prince of demons look like?

An angel of light.

When humans encounter this master of treachery, they think they have encountered a messenger of beauty and truth.

This verse is the conclusion of a longer argument. Paul writes, "And no wonder!" Why does he say this?

He says this because, in context, he is talking about his

profound concern that his friends *who knew the Lord* would be seduced away from the simple gospel of the grace of God, and the clear teachings of the Word of God.

> For I am jealous for you with godly jealousy. For I have betrothed you to one husband, that I may present you as a chaste virgin to Christ. (2 Corinthians 11:2)

Every Christian is married to Christ, he says. By definition. The great miracle of the new birth immediately generates the closest union possible between the believer and Christ. The child of God is instantly purified, as a *chaste* virgin, and is made one with Christ.

The basis of that relationship is as secure as the triumph of the Crucified and Risen One.

But a believer's experience of that relationship is always on shaky ground.

It is on shaky ground because there is a ceaseless attack by countless seducers every single day.

- But I fear, lest somehow, as the serpent deceived Eve by his craftiness, so your minds may be corrupted from the simplicity that is in Christ. (2 Corinthians 11:3)
- For such are false apostles, deceitful workers, transforming themselves into apostles of Christ. And no wonder! For Satan himself transforms himself into an angel of light. (2 Corinthians 11:13, 14)

Paul styles these seducers "false apostles." They do not look like demon worshippers or sorcerers. Though they are incarnations of satanic lies, they present themselves with uncanny charm and irresistible appeal.

They look like workers for Jesus. When the people of God

observe them, we declare, *Wow, look at those wonderful servants of God!* Yet the great Apostle declares them to be "deceitful workers."

The diabolical charmer deceives whole nations. He deceives so many their number is "as the sand of the sea" (Revelation 20:7, 8). In fact, Paul says he "deceives the whole world" (Revelation 12:9).

The whole world.

Why are so many so utterly deceived?

Because the heart is deceitful and because biblical illiteracy is normal and because the devil is subtle. These somber realities combine to produce a drunken world, and a church too distracted, clueless, or co-opted to do anything about it.

Subtlety is simply the most forgotten, most forgettable, most overlooked reality of the malicious tyrant Satan as he operates in the world today.

He has had millennia to perfect the art of working incognito.

And we, because we are so biblically lame, and are as yet unweaned from the breast of subjectivity and emotion, are incapable of distinguishing between Satan's putrid lies and God's glorious truth.

THE DEVIL'S RAGE

What we see in the world today is the devil's rage. What we are seeing in culture, in arts, in politics, in media, on social media, in academia, and sadly in so many churches and from so many pulpits is mass hypnosis. It is mass hallucination, courtesy the wicked angel of light.

The devil is a gorgeous con artist. From a biblical standpoint, it is not an exaggeration to say he has conned the whole wide stupefied world. He has spewed his acid spit everywhere. He has done so in the name of *all that is good*—in politics, social justice, arts, media, entertainment, and academia.

But solid food belongs to those who are of full age, *that is,* those who by reason of use have their senses exercised to discern both good and evil. (Hebrews 5:14)

Translation: we Christians are insanely quick to embrace as good that which God calls evil. We are clueless, because we are essentially starved of the "solid food" of deep theology.

In a perverse sense of the love of Christ, we flock to every social movement no matter how corrupt its foundations. We "stand with" every moral deviancy, we overlook any theological heresy, we embrace every category called oppressed no matter how anti-biblical their methods. We latch onto the novel and the passionate. We march for a so-called justice neither Jesus nor the apostles ever endorsed — all of this under the smiling approval of his infernal majesty, the devil. The church is heavily populated—indeed it is largely run—by spiritual babies incapable of discerning good and evil.

In too many cases to count, where the duped people of God rush to something they deem beautiful, God in heaven urgently wants them to spot the fanged smile of the drooling devil.

Cut it out. Stop it. Grow up. Have a little discernment.

It's the devil, stupid.

In the face of this, I am staggered by the claim of Jesus when he told his disciples, "I give you authority... over all the power of the enemy" (Luke 10:19).

Just before that he said, "I saw Satan fall like lightning from heaven" (Luke 10:18).

This is a remarkable reminder. We have no time for pessimism. We have no excuse for giving up.

Jesus has delegated to us his own authority and power. He has made his victory our victory. He has reminded us that our fight is not primarily political, or philosophical, or cultural, or social justice, or against flesh and blood.

We have been given a surplus of supernatural divine resources to put this cunning foe to shame. Our marching orders are clear: go on in this strength of the Master, and win the world to Jesus.

MARCHING ORDERS

Toward the end of his life, the great missionary and church planter and theology expert of the church, the Apostle Paul, went on trial before the Roman ruler of Palestine, King Herod Agrippa II.

Paul was on trial for his life—a time when we might choose our words carefully.

Paul shares the testimony of his shocking realization that this Jesus Christ, whom he persecuted, was Lord of All, the unrivaled Master and Commander of the universe.

Then Paul makes a remarkable statement, summing up in a single verse, a clearly articulated MISSION STATEMENT for his entire ministry and life. God was sending him to the nations—

> ...to open their eyes, in order to turn them from darkness to light, and from the power of Satan to God, that they may receive forgiveness of sins and an inheritance among those who are sanctified by faith in [Jesus.]' (Acts 26:18)

Paul envisioned the nations of the world as caught in the grip of Satan. He visited city after city, village after village. In every case the situation was clear. The people he met in the marketplace and malls, the people he debated in schools and homes, the people he taught in synagogues and churches, they were—one and all—trapped by Satan.

Compounding the problem was the fact they didn't realize it, and denied it when told.

So it is today, both in culture and, sadly, in the church. This was everything to Paul. This was the main thing. This was the only thing. Opening blind eyes, and turning hypnotized people from the power of Satan to God.

The burden of this book, and of my heart, is, that on the deepest levels, absolutely nothing has changed for us today.

The devil is equally cunning.

Our neighbors and friends and family—the people we work with, and go to school with, and golf with—are equally spellbound and blind.

Those who do not know the Lord, no matter how loving and decent and woke and active in the church, are still in desperate and urgent need to turn from Satan, from the same serpent that beguiled Eve. Every single person who does not know the Lord remains today in a condition of desperate and urgent need to turn from Satan to God.

But they don't know it.

If we, in the church do not know it either, all hope is lost. This culpable ignorance among God's own people is the root of all our chaos.

We are tinkering with behaviors when only a new heart will do.

Only the gospel of Jesus Christ has the power to deliver people from the heartbreak, nihilism, despair, violence, hedonism, and all the broken philosophies of a society hellbent on erasing God from their knowledge.

The most cunning schemes of the devil will evaporate into nothingness before the preaching of the Cross of Christ.

LOOK BENEATH THE SURFACE

> But even if our gospel is veiled, it is veiled to those who are perishing, whose minds the god of this age [Satan] has blinded, who do not believe, lest the light of the gospel of the glory of Christ, who is the image of God, should shine on them. (2 Corinthians 4:3, 4)

We are not just dealing with differing opinions. We are not

just dealing with contradictory worldviews, or with left and right and conservative and liberal.

We are dealing with a stupor and a moral drunkenness induced by the devil. The god of this age has blinded them. The devil is nothing to them. And the gospel is as irrelevant to them as a fairy tale from childhood.

Look beneath the surface.

Look beneath the surface in the world.

Those social media posts that drive you crazy? Those political decisions that make no sense? Those conflicts of race, those redefinitions of history, those financial issues, everything that you see in media and music and movies and art? It's all DUI. It's all under the influence of Satan.

There is "strong delusion" across the land.

People are believing a lie.

Look beneath the surface.

Beneath the surface of all this chaos is spiritual warfare.

Beneath the surface of violence and evil is spiritual warfare.

Beneath the surface of divisiveness on media is spiritual warfare.

Beneath the surface of narcissism on social media is spiritual warfare.

Beneath the anarchy and hatred of authority, beneath the insurrection, beneath the racism, beneath the violence against police, beneath the corruption in politics, beneath the perversion of holy sexuality, beneath the redefinition of marriage, male, female, and life itself... beneath it all is the smiling and composed face of the most attractive, destructive, seductive, spiteful, hateful malevolent being the world has ever known.

Look beneath the surface in the church too.

Why is the Word of God set on the sidelines among the people of God? Why the constant battle against theological drift? Why are we turning for truth to experience and emotion, rather than to the inerrant Scriptures? Why has worship music become so bland, and the doctrine of hell so forgotten, and the path of holiness so muddy and obscure?

In all these things, we are not wrestling with flesh and blood. The devil is feasting on our minds.

Why the pandemic legalism? Why the confusion over the most basic truths of the gospel? Why the utter indifference to the return of the Lord? Why are we redefining Christian growth, and turning disciple-making into worldly behavior modification? Why are we more interested in inspirational leadership than in expositional labor? In niceness rather than truth?

Why are the cross of Christ, and the doctrines of salvation, tiny specks on the horizon, when they should be in the foreground of the church's consciousness?

Why the chaos in the world and in the church today?

It's the devil, stupid.

Look beneath the surface.

There is no need to scratch our heads. No need to assemble a committee to study the problem.

"Now the serpent was more cunning than any beast of the field." This is the fundamental truth we forget at our peril.

But on a deeper level, it's much more true that the weapons of our warfare are not of human origin, but they are mighty in God.

The church's greatest struggle will always be the cunning devil coupled with the calloused heart.

But our greatest asset, and our undeniable victory, will always be the Satan-crushing gospel, the razor sharp sword of the Word of God, and the consecrated church willing to go into all the world to proclaim the dynamic, powerful, and all-sufficient message of the blood-bought grace of God.

When these all sufficient supernatural divine resources are put into to play, the devil doesn't stand a chance. It's time to turn the spotlight. It's time to look up, and to see the Lord Almighty, sitting on his throne, laughing at his adversaries, and blessing his saints. He's got it all under control. Let us now turn our attention from the chaos of the world to the unstoppable force of God working in the world today through grace and truth, bringing a peace only he can deliver.

PART 2
THE REVIVAL WE NEED

WHEN LUTHER NAILED his 95 Theses to the Wittenburg Door, he threw the first punch in a *doctrinal* fight. It was not Luther's objective to split the church. He only wanted to correct the ship's doctrinal course, and to return the Church to her most fundamental truths such as justification by faith and the authority of Scripture.

This triggered an epic brawl scholars call the Protestant Reformation.

It is Protestant because it flowed out of Luther's protest against the false teaching and excesses of the church.

It is a Reformation because it unburied important theological structures from an avalanche of ecclesiastical, political, and theological debris.

Reformation has to do mainly with theology and doctrine. The Protestant Reformation also happened to trigger a Revival, but let's save that for the final chapters.

The first urgent requirement to deliver the church from her chaotic condition is a thoroughgoing theological Reformation. We stand in desperate need of a penitent return to the Bible and our first principles.

Here's our working definition of Reformation:

Reformation is the work of God as he rebuilds the biblical foundations of the church, tears down demonic structures of deception and error, and restores the authority of Scripture and the knowledge of the gospel among his own people.

I would like to devote this chapter to restoration of the authority of Scripture, and the next chapter to the restoration of the knowledge of the gospel.

THE AUTHORITY OF SCRIPTURE

For Luther, the tug of war was between the Authority of Scripture vs. the Teaching Magisterium of the Catholic Church. "A simple layman armed with Scripture is to be believed above a pope or a council without it."[1] Fighting words.

Today's tug of war is different. On one side stands the Authority of Scripture. On the other stand all the forces that would topple Scripture from its epistemological throne. These would include empiricism, rationalism, irrationalism, nihilism, emotionalism, subjectivism, hedonism, pragmatism, and a diabolical host of other -isms.

These boil down to a ceaseless tug of war between two possible sources of ultimate truth. Source one: ME. Source two: NOT ME.

When we take our stand on the authority of Scripture, we are saying that the source of Ultimate Truth is found, not by looking within, but by looking to an external authority, i.e., the pages of Scripture.

When we take our stand on any other source, we are saying that we find truth by looking within and deciding what structure of reality best comports with our subjective opinion. This, in effect, makes us our own gods. "In those days there was no king in Israel; everyone did what was right in his own eyes" (Judges 17:6).

That must have been a very weird time to be alive.

So it is today. It's a very weird time to be alive.

Post-modernism has made truth into a choose-your-own buffet. Look within for what resonates. Put that on your plate. Enjoy.

The first reformation must be epistemological.

Where do we get our truth? I know I am only echoing a thousand other voices, but for some reason the echo keeps fading.

How can we shout this to a church caught in a maelstrom of conflicting ideologies?

- In a culture built on Reason, the church could make the case for Scripture based on reason. Logic. Presuppositions. Apologetics.
- In a culture built on Emotion, the church might make its case based on emotion — that there has never been a more life-giving, emotionally healthy worldview than biblical Christianity. Jesus Christ and his message radiate a beauty and social goodness unparalleled in the annals of human thought.
- In a culture built on Empiricism, we might argue that the five senses had to come from somewhere, and that the whole house of science is built on a leap of faith that our observations are telling us the truth.
- In a culture built on Irrationality, we probably need a combination of joy, sarcasm, good stories, and pithy aphorisms, joined to a sacrificial love. A lot like Jesus. In the end, irrationality is a painful way to live, and its adherents will soon be looking for a better way.

I am saying that, viewed from the standpoint of *any* ideology, a decent apologetic can still make the case for the supremacy of Scripture. Biblical Epistemology wins.

THE POWER OF THE GOSPEL

In any event, the main thing remains that we proclaim Christ. We are called to teach, preach, share, and gossip the gospel. The good news is that the Holy Spirit goes wherever the gospel goes, no matter what kind of audience we're talking to.

Scripture packs its own power. If we put it out there wisely, and frame it lovingly, it can still blast through the devil's deceptions with ease.

Sadly, however, from the modernism of the twentieth century, to the seekerism/consumerism of the twenty-first, to the subjectivism of today, the doctrinal package called the gospel has largely warmed the bench, waiting to be called into the game. "You're just basing all that on the Bible. Who says that is true?"

I am not surprised when the world says this. I am almost crushed when the church says it.

Consider the problem of "theological drift" at some of our more influential evangelical colleges and universities. I am not saying that these institutions are losing the battle for the Bible. I am just saying the battle is raging in places a previous generation considered immune. Thankfully, most, if not all, of these schools are doing their best to stand strong.

- A long-time trustee of Asuza Pacific University voiced concerns that APU is struggling with a "theological drift from what is required of an evangelical Christian university." Two members of the board of trustees have resigned over the issue.[2]
- Moody Bible Institute, that bastion of theological conservatism, recently implemented a requirement that faculty subscribe to the Chicago Statement on Biblical Inerrancy. Some chaos has arisen over a couple of professors who expressed their divergence from what is called the "correspondence theory" of truth — the self-evident

idea that truth is reality and reality is truth. In response, the administration has instituted this new requirement. Some faculty members in the Bible and theology departments resent the new requirement, because it "wounds" them. [3] Honest to God?

- In 2018, a group of professors at Taylor University launched a theologically conservative newspaper called *Excalibur*. They were trying to balance what they saw as a liberal leaning movement at the university. "We are Taylor University faculty, staff, and students who heartily affirm the historic orthodox theological doctrines, as expressed in the Apostles creed and other classical ecumenical creeds." They voiced a concern that existing school publications "offer[ed] insufficient means to counter leftist trends." Pressure from faculty, administration, and students led to the publication's rapid abandonment. [4]

- Shockwaves shook evangelicalism when a Wheaton College professor announced that "Christians and Muslims worship the same God." The professor was separated from employment, but not without a massive blowup inside the school and in the media.

- A 2014 meeting of the Evangelical Theological Society featured a panel discussion on challenges to biblical inerrancy facing Christian colleges and seminaries. "The doctrine of Scripture is like a continental divide," Greg Wills, Southern Baptist Theological Seminary's dean of theology, said during a panel discussion. He correctly pointed out, "Your doctrine of Scripture is not like one doctrine in a basket full of doctrines; it's the doctrine that determines which basket full of doctrines you have." [5]

My point is not to criticize these institutions, as each one is actually fighting for "the faith once delivered to the saints." I am simply pointing out that the fight is everywhere, even within our most cherished evangelical institutions.

Postmodernism, the opiate of liberal theologians, has stretched its tentacles everywhere.

The consequence is the chaos we see.

BACK TO THE BIBLE

I argued earlier that we need our scholars. But we need scholars who buttress, not batter, the church's faith. This requires epistemological repentance. The Bible, rightly interpreted in its plain sense, has the final say in everything we believe.

This is of utmost importance. Without this, the church continues a slide into accommodationism and, ultimately, irrelevancy.

Francis Schaeffer, please come back. We desperately need your message:

> It is the central things of the Word of God which make Christianity Christianity. These we must hold tenaciously, and, even when it is costly for us and even when we must cry, we must maintain that there is not only an antithesis of truth, but an antithesis that is observable in practice. Out of a loyalty to the infinite-personal God who is there and who has spoken in Scripture, and out of compassion for our own young people and others, we who are evangelicals dare not take a halfway position concerning truth or the practice of truth.[6]

> Here is the great evangelical disaster — the failure of the evangelical world to stand for truth as truth. There is only one word for this — namely accommodation: the evangelical church has accommodated to the world spirit of the age.[7]

We will stand for truth only when we stand unashamedly, and unapologetically, on the Bible as both true and real. As Schaeffer put it, "true truth." No evasions. No Jedi mind-tricks to erode its authority. No modern-day prophets, or Apostles, or Super-Apostles. Just an old-fashioned religion based on the face-value interpretation of the Word of God as The Word of God.

Only this "faith once delivered to the saints" is sufficient to defeat the spirit of the age. And make no mistake, the spirit of the age is a spiteful monster, hellbent on wiping the Christian truth-claim from the face of the earth, and Christians along with it. It is a spirit belched from the gut of the Dragon himself.

But it comes dressed in tolerant, loving, appealing theological garb. The devil is subtle. He smiles winsomely, shakes your hand, and says, "I'm the Angel of Light. I'm here to help."

With his other hand, he stabs the Church in the back.

A church ignorantly swept up in today's pandemonium, populated by sincere, activistic, sentimental, emotionally worshipful, but still stunted, Christians, will be the end of us.

Why?

Because the church urgently needs a backbone of theological steel forged in Scripture, not in the philosophical word games of the day. And not in a piety whipped up by manipulative apostles and prophets of God. If we surrender truth, we surrender morality. If we surrender morality, we surrender human dignity and it's game over.

Luther said, "Unless I am convicted by Scripture and by plain reason, I do not accept the authority of popes and councils, for they have contradicted each other. My conscience is captive to the Word of God. I cannot and will not recant anything, for to go against conscience is neither right nor safe. Here I stand. I cannot do otherwise. God help me."

May God multiply his tribe.

A child of God armed with Scripture, is mightier than an Ivy League professor armed with deconstructionism.

Such a believer packs more punch than the adrenaline rush

of a gut-wrenching, theologically insipid worship song. They are more impactful than a legion of do-gooders, "loving on" people, but leaving them in their sins. And more frightening to Satan's hordes than the charismatic pastor plucking the church's heartstrings with simplistic platitudes.

We need the Bible.

We need the Bible in its fulness and breadth and depth.

We need the people of God to find their truth in the Bible.

We need the pastors and preachers and professors of the church to revere the Bible and its truth as the singular, non-negotiable, irreplaceable doorway to the knowledge of God.

We need our teachers to organize the Bible into digestible units through the use of technical vocabulary and the correct application of Theology Proper.

We need to set emotion and experience and encounters and signs and wonders and sentimentality and activity and service and love and all the mush of human emotion some-where far below the Bible in importance as our source for truth.

We need to go deep into the Bible. We need the vocabulary of faith. We need times in which we set aside our paraphrases — our simplified versions and dynamic equivalences — that we might unearth the technical words of God in Scripture, and upload them into our psyches.

We need theologically committed preachers more than inspiring and visionary leaders.

We need church leaders and church people who hold up a Bible and say, "Here is the truth," in the face of a nearly universal consensus that truth has already died.

We need depth in the pulpit and preachers who don't borrow their sermons. Uninformed clergy is killing us. Don't just reflect on the Scripture and drool out pabulum. Study the hell out of Scripture and then reflect on your studies.

We need a generation of Christians who, like their grand-parents, wear out their Bibles, digitally if need be.

We need to uphold the Bible as epistemologically sufficient

— abundant even — across the entire spectrum of human, societal, and cosmic need.

We need meat not milk. Exposition, not topics. Long form truth, not snippets.

Nothing else will do. Nothing else will satisfy the soul. Nothing else will paint a picture of a God so simultaneously awful and grace-full that he takes our breath away. Nothing else will uphold a blood-bought gospel of grace in a world itching for substitutes. Nothing else will imbue the human race with the dignity for which God designed it.

We need the Bible.

Desperately. Urgently. STAT!

Luther triggered a Reformation when he elevated Scripture above Popes.

May a new generation ignite a New Reformation by elevating Scripture above everything. Above emotion, subjectivism, depraved cultural norms, notions of social justice, "wokeness," peer pressure, preference, feelings, science, fake science, philosophy, visions, prophecies, dreams, new apostolic pronouncements, angelic visitations, majority opinion, and any other created thing.

Ecclesiastical chaos is the price of cheap epistemology. Let us repent and return to the Word of God in its fulness and depth, that we may find in its pages the smiling face of its Divine Author.

If the condition of the world depends on the condition of the church, there is no alternative. We need this Reformation. Urgently. Desperately. Only a Reformation that recovers the authority of Scripture packs the power to realign the church to reality. And only such a realignment in the church can initiate a movement in the world that can ease the chaos resulting from our cultural addiction to absurdity.

Finally only such a return to the authority of Scripture can properly elevate Jesus above the din of a world gone wild, restoring him to his rightful place as the sun of our epistemological solar system.

As the late James Montgomery Boice so eloquently said,

Some persons think they can know God by means of their own human reason. But reason is a blind ally spiritually. It has always been the great minds exercising their powers apart from the Word of God who have produced the great heresies. Some think they can discover God by listening to a so-called "inner voice." But the voice is often nothing more than an expression of their own inner desires. Quite a few think that spiritual truths can be verified by supernatural events or miracles. But the Bible everywhere teaches that even miracles will not lead men and women to understand and receive God's truth unless they themselves are illuminated by the Bible (see Luke 16:31). I believe that we can state categorically that there is no knowledge apart from Jesus Christ and that there is no knowledge of Jesus Christ apart from a knowledge of the Bible.[8]

1. Cited in Roland H. Bainton, *Here I Stand: A Life of Martin Luther* (Peabody, MA: Hendrickson, 2010), 180.
2. Samuel Smith, in *The Christian Post*. "Azusa Pacific's new president to promote 'unity' amid concerns of 'theological drift'" on April 17, 2019 at https://www.christianpost.com/news/azusa-pacifics-new-president-to-promote-unity-amid-concerns-of-theological-drift.html
3. Julie Roys. "Moody Professors Protest: Will Sign Chicago Statement but it 'Means Nothing to Me'" at Julie Roys, http://julieroys.com/moody-professors-protest-will-sign-chicago-statement-means-nothing/ retrieved March 27, 2019.
4. Anthony Gockowski in Campus Reform, "Conservative paper pressured into suspending publication" March 21, 2018 retrieved from https://www.campusreform.org/?ID=10670.
5. Keith Collier in The Biblical Recorder, "Inerrancy drift festers in Christian academia," Jan. 9, 2017 at https://www.brnow.org/news/Inerrancy-drift-festers-in-Christian-academia/ retrieved Jul 19, 2020.
6. (Francis A. Schaeffer, The Church at the End of the Twentieth Century, Ch. 1)
7. (Francis A. Schaeffer, The Church at the End of the Twentieth Century, Ch. 1)
8. Retrieved from Grace Quotes, July 3, 2020 at https://gracequotes.org/topic/bible-sufficiency/

YOU COULD SMELL THE SWEAT, the discomfort in the class-room. Pastors-in-training, some of them in the employ of my own church, sat in my classroom at a local Christian college. It was time for an exam. An oral exam. A bit of Socratic tough love for an easy A.

"Sam, tell me what justification means," I said.

My student blushed and looked around vainly for help. "Um... being made righteous?"

"Oh," I said, "so after a person is justified, their lives are immediately righteous, and they start doing good things, right?"

"Um... no?"

"Tony, help Sam out," I said, letting Sam off the hook.

"After you're saved you're supposed to do good works," he said.

"So, we teach salvation by works, is that what you mean?" I said.

"No, no. Um, it's like, well, like..."

These were Bible majors in a Christian college. Juniors and seniors. Most of this particular group had grown up in Christian homes, attending youth groups and church on a regular basis.

Yet none of them could articulate what is arguably the

single most important doctrine in the salvation-package, the doctrine of justification by faith — the very doctrine that revolutionized the life and impact of Martin Luther.

To be more specific, my students were unable to articulate the difference between being *made* righteous and being *declared* righteous, the very wedge that Luther would use to unintentionally split the church.

> Night and day I pondered until I saw the connection between the justice of God and the statement that 'the just shall live by his faith.' Then I grasped that the justice of God is that righteousness by which through grace and sheer mercy God justifies us through faith. Thereupon I felt myself to be reborn and to have gone through open doors into paradise.
>
> - MARTIN LUTHER

> Justification is the main hinge on which salvation turns.
>
> - JOHN CALVIN

Knowing the centrality of justification, I have made exploring this doctrine a huge part of most of my classes for aspiring ministers. It is a foundational doctrine. Just as cracks in a wall point to a shifting foundation, so chaos in the church points to a defective doctrine of justification.

Why?

Imagine being the proud owner of a vintage car. A friend suggests spending some time tinkering under the hood. A few days later, you're checking fluids together, setting the points, adjusting the timing, and tuning things up. Your friend points to the carburetor and says, "Let's yank that thing out."

You immediately object. "The car can't run without a carburetor! Besides, that thing is bolted to the engine, and it connects with pretty much every other system under the hood. Friends don't let friends mess with carburetors!"

Friends don't let friends mess with the doctrine of justification by faith either.

The doctrine of justification by faith is bolted tightly to the engine of Scripture. It interconnects with the doctrine of God, the doctrine of human nature, the doctrine of Christ, of salvation, of the church, and even of eschatology.

When they identified justification by faith as the paramount doctrine of the Reformation, Luther and Calvin identified the one doctrine that makes all the other doctrines go.

Unless we are crystal clear on this doctrine, we will muddy the waters of salvation, defame the character of God, fracture the stability of the church, and create a doctrinal vacuum that will suck in all sorts of error and chaos.

CATHOLICS AND PROTESTANTS TOGETHER

What do evangelical heavyweights of yesteryear, such as Charles Colson, Pat Robertson, J.I. Packer, and Bill Bright have in common with Catholic theologians including Peter Kreeft and Cardinal John O'Connor of New York?

They are all signatories of a 1994 ecumenical screed called "Evangelicals and Catholics Together"[1] — which was then praised by the evangelical mother ship, *Christianity Today*.[2]

Criticisms flew fast and furious from R.C. Sproul, John MacArthur, John Ankerberg, and a host of others. I believe rightly so.

I am Italian. Not only do I eat well, but I also have many Catholic family members and friends. I love them dearly. Many are saved, which is wonderful. I often say, "If you are going to be Baptist, be a saved Baptist. If you are going to be Catholic, be a saved Catholic. If you are going to be [insert Christian denomination here]" — you get the idea.

Even so, the Catholic Church has never rescinded its official denunciation, affirmed at the Council of Trent, of

Luther's teaching. Here are some notable examples of that feisty declaration of A.D. 1563. As you read, for the word *anathema*, substitute the word *damned*, and you'll catch the flavor.

> If any one saith, that the justice received is not preserved and also increased before God through good works; but that the said works are merely the fruits and signs of Justification obtained, but not a cause of the increase thereof; let him be anathema.

Translation: you're saved by works, not by faith alone, and if you disagree, to hell with you.

> If any one saith, that men are justified, either by the sole imputation of the justice of Christ, or by the sole remission of sins, to the exclusion of the grace and the charity which is poured forth in their hearts by the Holy Ghost, and is inherent in them; or even that the grace, whereby we are justified, is only the favour of God; let him be anathema.

Translation: you'd better be a really good person, and grace alone can't save you, and, by the way, stop arguing with this, or double damn you!

> If any one saith, that by faith alone the impious is justified; in such wise as to mean, that nothing else is required to co-operate in order to the obtaining the grace of Justification, and that it is not in any way necessary, that he be prepared and disposed by the movement of his own will; let him be anathema.

Translation: okay, yes to faith, but yes to works too, or just go to hell already.

This is official Catholic doctrine. It is the opposite of evangelical doctrine, and intentionally so. That is why the Council of Trent met in the first place. It's called the Counter Reformation for a reason.

While there are many points of agreement between Catholics and Evangelicals, some points of disagreement are, by any rational standard, insurmountable. This is why the 1994 document produced immediate controversy.

In fairness to the writers, they did enumerate significant differences that remained between Catholics and Evangelicals. They even state, "We reject any appearance of harmony that is purchased at the price of truth."[3]

But they proceed to sacrifice truth on the altar of harmony. They go so far as to suggest it is better for us to get along and cooperate in "the enormous challenge of our common evangelistic task" than to argue with each other's positions, or try to "proselytize" from each other's camps.

But wait. How can we have "a common evangelistic task" if we are preaching different gospels? If the way of salvation is at stake, isn't it worth fighting for? If the source of all truth is at stake, shouldn't we fight for that too? I don't care what church you're in, if you're not saved, my job is to proselytize you. No apologies.

Why do I bring this up?

I bring this up because the same impulse toward harmony and love that propelled this document to front page news a quarter century ago still molests the church today. The same truths remain points of contention — however, the front has shifted. It is no longer simply a Catholic/Evangelical divide. Now, it is an Evangelical/Evangelical divide too.

Whether in Luther's day, or in the era of "Catholics and Evangelicals Together," or in our post-emergent, post-modern moment, the truths under contention are still the same. Those truths are the authority of Scripture (*Sola Scriptura*) and the doctrine of Justification by Faith (*Sola Fide*).

Apparently, the devil has two demonic SWAT teams — one to poison discussions of epistemology, and the other to spew acid spit upon discussions about the way of salvation.

If we don't get these two doctrines right, we won't get anything right. So let's consider them both, starting with justification.

Justification is first and foremost an act of God. God does something by his wisdom, power, justice, and love. We are the beneficiaries. What does God do?

God declares a believing sinner to be righteous. That's what he does. It is the most counterintuitive proposition in the world. God finds a smelly, ragged, guilty sinner who only believes, and declares before the Supreme Court of the Cosmos that said sinner is officially righteous in the eyes of God.

This makes the devil spitting mad. It also makes legalists spitting mad, for similar reasons.

The key word is "declaration."

One of the first verses I memorized as a kid in my Awana days was Romans 4:5, quoted here as I learned it in the old King James Version: "But to him that worketh not, but believeth on him that justifieth the ungodly, his faith is counted for righteousness."

The operative phrase here denominates God as the one who "justifies the ungodly." To say that God justifies the ungodly is to state an oxymoron, were it not for the wisdom and grace of God.

The other operative phrase announces that such a person's "faith is counted for righteousness," where *counted* is the Greek term for a forensic or financial imputation.

The fact that I could not easily convey to my class of pastors-in-the-making was the distinction between being *declared* righteous and being *made* righteous. The day after your salvation, you are pretty much just as nasty as you were the day before your salvation. If salvation meant being *made* righteous, that behavior would instantly change.

But God never promised such an instantaneous change.

He said he would *declare* you righteous, not *make* you righteous in that moment. It is a matter of standing in the law books of heaven, not of behavior on earth. Catholics anathematize this idea. They argue that you are *made* righteous, or — to get theological — that righteousness is *imparted*, not *imputed*. Justification is a change of behavior, they say, not just of status, and it is the change of behavior that saves you.

Really? Isn't that salvation by works? Isn't that what the Reformers fought against?

This position suffers the fatal error of confusing *justification* with post-salvation *sanctification*, and always results in a legalistic, works-based salvation.

One of many nails in the coffin of this error is 2 Corinthians 5:21: "For He made Him who knew no sin to be sin for us, that we might become the righteousness of God in Him."

Paul is drawing a parallel between how our sins were placed on Christ and how Christ's righteousness was placed on us.

So let's ask how our sins were placed on Christ.

Did he go out and do sinful things? Was Jesus sinful *in his behavior?*

No. Never. Instead, our sins were *imputed* to Christ in the books of heaven — a credit to an account — though he always remained the sinless, spotless Lamb of God in behavior.

If that is how our sins were placed on Christ, it is also how his righteousness was placed on us. We can state this theologically too. Just as our sins were imputed, not imparted, to Christ, so his righteousness was imputed, not imparted, to us in the act of justification.

Read it again: "For He made Him who knew no sin to be sin for us, that we might become the righteousness of God in Him" (2 Corinthians 5:21).

- JUST AS OUR SINS WERE IMPUTED, NOT
IMPARTED, TO CHRIST, SO HIS RIGHTEOUSNESS WAS
IMPUTED, NOT IMPARTED, TO US.

We didn't run around and do good stuff. Rather, the good stuff of Christ, i.e., his inexhaustible supply of perfect divine righteousness was credited to our accounts in the books of heaven. Imputed, not imparted. Imputed, not infused.

- Romans 4:5: faith is counted [imputed] for righteousness
- Romans 4:6: God imputes righteousness apart from works
- Romans 4:11: that righteousness may be imputed to them also
- Romans 4:24: it shall be imputed to us also who believe in him

The writers of Scripture make it clear that justification is a divine declaration of our righteous standing before God, based solely on the imputed righteousness of Christ.

When did this happen? At the moment of faith — our "faith is counted for righteousness."

So, in the nano-second that you put your faith in Christ crucified and risen again, all the machinery of justification did its thing, and you didn't even feel it!

Your sins were imputed to Christ and paid for.

Christ's righteousness was imputed to you and recognized.

The Judge of Heaven and Earth turned his gaze your way, saw you standing in the shimmering robes of Christ's righteousness, and declared you utterly, perfectly, and irrevocably righteous forever and evermore — all this while you were still a mess in word, thought, and deed. This declaration was not based one whit on your behavior, but on the freely given, imputed righteousness of Christ.

[That I may] be found in Him, not having my own righteousness, which is from the law, but that which is through faith in Christ, the righteousness which is from God by faith. (Philippians 3:9)

Some theologians call this "forensic" justification, emphasizing its legal aspect in the court of heaven.[4]

Imputed righteousness is the discovery that awakened Luther. It is a discovery that changed my life in a sweaty high school gym my junior year. It is the discovery I was aiming for in that sweaty classroom of future pastors. It is the discovery I am after in the church today.

If the imparted-righteousness position is correct, we can never be certain of our salvation. We can never know if we have done enough good works to merit salvation.

Even the lame argument that our righteous deeds are motivated or enabled by grace doesn't solve anything. This position flies in the face of countless scriptural statements wiping works, law, deeds of the law, and any human effort off the table once for all. Works play no part whatsoever in the obtaining of eternal salvation. To claim otherwise is to deny Scripture, to insult the cross of Christ, to nullify his cry "IT IS FINISHED," and to welcome salvation by works in the back door after shoving it out the front door.

If the gospel isn't Christ alone, it isn't good news.

The doctrine of justification by faith alone in Christ alone will always be scandalous to people who don't get it, and to erase the scandal is to drop a grenade into the engine of salvation.

A FRONT END LOADED PROPOSITION

God's gift of salvation remains forever a front end loaded proposition. You get everything the day you believe. You are blessed with "every spiritual blessing" at the moment of faith (Ephesians 1:3). God's divine power has granted you "all things" that pertain to life and godliness on day one of your salvation (2 Peter 1:3).

Christian living is not about getting more stuff from God. It is not about chasing his blessing. It is not about meriting anything from God at all.

Justification by faith is God's shout to the universe that God's children do not serve him *for* blessing, but *from* blessing.

It is God's great declaration that you are good enough for heaven even if you never do one good thing in your life, because that is the strength of the imputed righteousness of Christ.

Justification is divine permission to live with nothing left to prove. You don't have to prove yourself to your father, your mother, your skeptical teachers, or your dissatisfied ex-, children, boss, pastor, priest, or pope. God has announced to angels, demons, the devil, and the saints in heaven that you are perfect in his sight. Who cares what anyone else thinks?

Justification can never be an attainment of works. It is an obtainment of faith.

By definition, a Christian is a person who has received "the gift of righteousness" (Romans 5:17). Theologians call this an "alien" righteousness, because it comes from a source other than yourself.

> I will greatly rejoice in the LORD, My soul shall be joyful in my God; For He has clothed me with the garments of salvation, He has covered me with the robe of righteousness, As a bridegroom decks himself with ornaments, And as a bride adorns herself with her jewels. (Isaiah 61:10)

Only the perfect righteousness of Christ will do.

> *My hope is built on nothing less*
> *Than Jesus' blood and righteousness;*
> *I dare not trust the sweetest frame,*
> *But wholly lean on Jesus' name.*
>
> *When he shall come with trumpet sound,*
> *O may I then in him be found,*
> *Dressed in his righteousness alone,*
> *Faultless to stand before the throne.*

On Christ, the solid rock, I stand;
All other ground is sinking sand,
All other ground is sinking sand.

- EDWARD MOTE, 1834

SO WHAT?

Why is justification so important for reformation and revival?

Justification is important because the mother of all chaos is confusion over the gospel.

Justification is important because sloppiness over the way of salvation multiplies chaos in the church, which multiplies chaos in the world.

Justification is important because we are supposed to read our Bibles with precision and care, and the failure to do so — whether through ignorance, apathy, laziness, or the desire to get along — makes everyday Christians conclude the whole theological endeavor is a waste of time, so let's just "love on" each other.

It is important because justification by faith is a grown up doctrine, and growing up has been my burden all along. A correct knowledge of justification by faith will make an immediate seismic shift in our concept of everything that matters: sin, salvation, the Cross, grace, faith, heaven, theology proper, anthropology, your own psychology, your assurance of eternal life, your everyday Christian life, and the church's mission on planet earth.

There is no measure to the harm done to the church by our persistent muddying of the gospel waters. Evangelism has all but perished in the western world and evangelists have withered away with it. By conflating justification with sanctification we have shuttered the birthing rooms of the church. We have recreated the conditions that led Luther to nail his complaints to the Wittenburg Door.

Justification by faith, deeply held, heals damaged emotions.

It delivers from legalism. It enables a life with nothing left to prove. "Who shall bring a charge against God's elect? It is God who justifies" (Romans 8:33).

To grasp justification is to grasp the *why* of evangelism. To grasp justification by faith is to grasp the *how* of evangelism. To grasp justification by faith alone in Christ alone is to grasp the *wow* of evangelism too.

A person is either justified by faith or damned.

Such binary thinking would go a long way toward sharpening the focus of the church.

If I could wave my magic wand, I would require every person at any level of Christian leadership to articulate the doctrine of justification by faith, and to differentiate righteousness *imputed* from righteousness *imparted*. That is the only way to pull up our ecclesiastical big kid pants. It is our only way to clear the chaos over both Scripture and salvation.

In other words, along with biblical authority, justification by faith remains the non-negotiable doctrinal catalyst for a New Reformation, which in turn is the only foundation for a Revival that actually means something.

We have to get our heads right before we light our hearts on fire. Justification is a great place to start. It worked for Paul. It worked for Luther. It will work for us today.

Faith alone. Grace alone. Scripture alone. Christ alone. Oh please, oh please, oh please, oh please.

Yes, I will still have uncomfortable dialogs in my pastoral classes. I will continue challenging the pandemic of fuzzy thinking over the gospel. I will push any applicant for ordination to make the case for forensic justification. And I will do my best to teach my church — and anyone who will listen — the wonders of an instantaneous transformation in status with God, that when understood and embraced, will change the mind, the heart, and yes, eventually, the life.

1. You can read the entire text here: https://www.firstthings.com/article/1994/05/evangelicals-catholics-together-the-christian-mission-in-the-third-millennium retrieved April 3, 2019.
2. Timothy George, "Catholics and Evangelicals in the Trenches," *Christianity Today* 38/6 (May 16, 1994) 16.
3. Paragraph 4
4. See the excellent case for this forensic justification in the essay *Forensic Justification*, by 16th century theologian Francis Turretin, here: https://www.ligonier.org/learn/articles/forensic-justification/

HISTORIANS GENERALLY AGREE on three Great Awakenings in the United States, often coinciding with revival in Europe. Let's review the American versions.

THE FIRST GREAT AWAKENING, 1740-1742

The first pilgrims to America were strong believers in Christ. They saw America as a new promised land and determined to establish a society founded upon the Word of God.

Unfortunately, as time went on, the spiritual enthusiasm of the pilgrims declined. An increase in wealth, a new generation unfamiliar with persecution, and an almost over-familiarity with things of Christ began to blunt the spiritual edge of society. By 1679, a group of pastors met in Boston to discuss "the necessity of reformation" and the evils that had "provoked the Lord to turn his judgements on New England." By the early 1700s a Boston preacher sadly observed, "Alas, as though nothing but the most amazing thunders and lightnings, and the most terrible earthquakes could awaken us, we are at this time fallen into as dead a sleep as ever."[1]

Into that bleak scene, God raised up a pastor named Jonathan Edwards. Edwards received his theological training at what would become Yale University. He entered the pastorate in the Congregational Church at Northhampton, Massachusetts. Edwards spent thirteen or fourteen hours per day in prayer and Bible study. Soon, God began to shake up his church with a spiritual awakening. In 1733, Edwards preached a series of sermons on — surprise, surprise — justification by faith. By the end of the year he wrote, "the Spirit of God began extraordinarily to set in."

God had begun something remarkable within the church, among true believers, God's own people. I would love to shout the fact that this remarkable revival was rooted in doctrinal preaching, and preaching on justification by faith — just as in the days of Luther.

The work of the Spirit in Edward's church was powerful. Edwards' sermons were detailed, doctrinal, weighty, and meaty. Google them. See for yourself.

He read his sermons from a manuscript, and was somewhat monotonous. Being nearsighted, Edwards was forced to hold a candle in one hand and to bend over his pulpit. Hardly the dynamic, charismatic visionary-leader-preacher, Edwards saw God affect his congregations mightily. Unbelievers present would cry out in agony of conscience as the Holy Spirit convicted them of sin. People would literally pass out. They would clutch their pews in desperation, terrified that God would split open the earth and swallow them to hell right then and there. So many people were saved that Edwards could write, "souls did as it were come by floods to Jesus Christ." Remarkably large numbers of people were saved.

And that's what makes it revival.

The revival spread throughout Massachusetts and into Connecticut. The revival peaked under the ministry of itinerant evangelist, George Whitefield. Whitefield preached to upwards of 20,000 listeners in open air campaigns.

Imagine the lung-power to project a voice to 20,000 people with no mics and amps and speakers.

Revival spread to Boston, churches were packed and

services were held in homes. Revival spread to New York, New Jersey, Pennsylvania, Maryland, and Virginia.

One of the fruits of the First Great Awakening was an uncustomary zeal for evangelism. Missionaries were sent out, and the first missions among Native Americans were launched. David Brainerd, who was saved in the revival, launched one such mission. Edwards himself eventually became a missionary among Native Americans.

Another fruit of the First Great Awakening was cooperation among denominations. Walls were broken down, and universities like Princeton were opened to prepare pastors for the expanding frontier.

A concern for justice was born, and slavery was abolished in England. John Wesley wrote an influential letter, praying for the day when "American slavery (the vilest that ever saw the sun) shall vanish away before the power of God." Abolition's seeds were sown in revival.

One final fruit was the spirit of liberty and freedom of conscience before the Lord that led directly to the War for Independence and the founding of our nation. This First Great Awakening guaranteed that the American Republic would rest on a biblical and Christian foundation.

Edwards wrote,

> There was scarcely a single person in the town, old or young, left unconcerned about the great things of the eternal world. Those who were wont to be the vainest and loosest; and those who had been most disposed to think, and speak slightly of vital and experimental [experiential] religion, were now generally subject to great awakenings. And the work of conversion was carried on in a most astonishing manner, and increased more and more; souls did, as it were, come by flocks to Jesus Christ.... [T]he town seemed to be full of the presence of God...[2]

THE SECOND GREAT AWAKENING, 1800-1825

The First Great Awakening, like all revivals, subsided, and churches returned to business as usual. America grew rapidly. The frontier pushed westward, and the leading edge was essentially lawless and irreligious. By the 1800's the rationalistic theories of Rousseau, Voltaire, Paine, and Locke were exercising tremendous influence. Thomas Paine predicted, "Christianity will be forgotten in thirty years."

Whereas previous generations at least demonstrated a reverence for God, with the rise of Rationalism, even that disappeared. The status of Christianity was low and depressed.

Does this stunted situation sound familiar?

The seminaries fared no better. Lyman Beecher, of Yale Divinity School, lamented the "college was in a most ungodly state. The college church was almost extinct. Most of the students were skeptical, and rowdies were plenty. Wine and liquors were kept in many rooms; intemperance, profanity, gambling, and licentiousness were common. . . . That was the day of the infidelity of the Tom Paine school. . . . most of the class before me were infidels and called each other Voltaire, Rousseau... etc., etc."

Another pastor wrote, "The state of religion is gloomy and distressing; the church of Christ seems to be sunk very low."

Christianity is never more than one generation from extinction.

Many pastors, aware of the desperate need for pastors on the expanding frontier, made it a priority to recapture Yale for Christ. A grandson of Jonathan Edwards was made president of Yale just before 1800. His name was Timothy Dwight. Yale was formed to train pastors, yet it had become the citadel of unbelief. Dwight turned all that around with his loving demeanor and his biblical preaching.

In 1802, Dwight led two influential seniors to Christ. They shared their testimony, and many other students came to Christ. Conviction multiplied, and young college students and future pastors were lit on fire for the Lord. Dwight feared that during the summer break, the awakening would fizzle out.

The opposite proved true.

As students fanned out across the land, they carried the story of an awakening at Yale. The spiritual awakening spread from Yale to Dartmouth, and soon after to Princeton. Eventually, even Harvard returned to its historic Christian roots. And a generation of young leaders were lit on fire by God. They would carry the spark of revival throughout the burgeoning countryside.

Can you imagine the Ivy Leagues again proclaiming the gospel of Christ? God did the impossible before. I'm praying he does it again.

The population was expanding at an unprecedented pace into Kentucky, Tennessee, Louisiana, and the West. New towns sprang up overnight. Eastern churches emptied out as congregants travelled west. How could the gospel of Christ possibly keep pace with the growth of the nation?

Only through revival, and that is exactly what God sent. The Second Great Awakening made the First Great Awakening look like a Sunday School picnic. The First Great Awakening lasted only three to five years. The Second Great Awakening lasted upwards of twenty-five years. The First Great Awakening was confined mostly to the eastern towns like Boston and Philadelphia. The Second Great Awakening affected both the eastern towns and the western frontier. One seminary president wrote,

> From the time I entered the College, in 1800, down to the year 1825, there was an uninterrupted series of these celestial visitations, spreading over different parts of the land. During the whole of these twenty-five years, there was not a month in which we could not point to some village, some city, some seminary of learning, and say: "Behold what hath God wrought."[3]

Camp Meetings

While in the East this revival was centered in the colleges and college towns, in the wild west, it was centered in "Camp Meetings." Camp Meetings were large gatherings at which people camped for days on end, and many preachers would fan out to preach in groups large and small. The most famous of these is the Cane Ridge camp meetings of August, 1801.

Situated in Logan County, Kentucky, the Cane Ridge meetings were held in the heart of spiritual darkness. Logan County was described as, "A Rogues Harbour." An observer wrote, "Here many refugees from almost all parts of the Union fled to escape justice or punishment. . . . Murderers, horse-thieves, highway robbers and counterfeiters fled here, until they combined and actually formed a majority." Laying the groundwork for the Cane Ridge Camp meetings, a circuit-riding preacher named James McCready preached directly to this rough and tumble audience.

He could speak of heaven so graphically that hard-hearted hearers would long to be there. When he preached of hell, one listener later recounted that McCready could "so array hell and its horrors before the wicked, that they would tremble and quake, imagining a lake of fire and brimstone yawning to overwhelm them, and the wrath of God thrusting them down to the horrible abyss."

After three years of ministry, McCready held meetings to unite the four or five hundred people in the churches on his circuit. He invited three other preachers to minister with him. The meetings were solemn and reverent, and it was obvious God was doing something among his people. On the final day, when one of the guest preachers was preaching, suddenly the people began to joyously and frantically shout and cry. The preacher, John McGee, was opposed to such displays of emotion and tried to stop them. The pastors as a group struggled against these manifestations. However, the pastors themselves began to feel an overwhelming power of God, such that they finally "acquiesced and stood in astonishment, admiring the wonderful works of God."

The meetings grew until, in 1801, estimates at the Cane Ridge meetings ranged from ten to twenty five thousand people. This is remarkable given the fact that the largest town in Kentucky only had 1,800 inhabitants. One report says, "The roads were crowded with wagons, carriages, horses, and footmen moving to the solemn camp."

Peter Cartwright

Perhaps the central figure in the west was a preacher named Peter Cartwright. He is the epitome of the rugged, circuit riding preacher. Saved at a Camp Meeting, Cartwright had no formal education. He began preaching at age sixteen, and kept at it for over forty years.

Being a circuit rider meant never knowing where you would sleep, having only a Bible and a hymnal for a library, and having to rough it up every once in a while. Cartwright reminisced, "We walked on dirt floors for carpets... had forked sticks and pocket-knives for knives and forks; slept on bear, deer, or buffalo skins before the fire, or sometimes on the ground in open air. One new suit of clothes of homespun was ample clothing for one year." It was a life of utter liberation coupled with poverty, accepted cheerfully.

It is reported that Cartwright had a booming voice. He could make strong men tremble and women weep. The wild West needed a strong figure, and Cartwright provided just that. He was a one-verse preacher, preaching countless times on John 1:29: "Behold the Lamb of God who takes away the sin of the world." Cartwright often had to resort to fistfights to quiet down the troublemakers in his crowds. For decades, Cartwright organized camp meetings throughout the west.

One of the manifestations under his preaching was something he called "the jerks."

No matter whether they were saints or sinners, they would

be suddenly captured by song or sermon and seized with a convulsive jerking all over, which they could not by any possibility avoid. The more they resisted, the more they jerked.

Cartwright tells how hats would go flying and he would fight hard to suppress his own laughter.

The Jerks

Now, what about the crying out, and the falling down, and the jerks, and other manifestations? Isn't that just a charismatic thing? Isn't that emotionalism? Let me quickly say that these manifestations in the Great Awakenings were not like what you might see on television today in big, enthusiastic or even charismatic Christian rallies. There were major differences.

First, the audience was different. In the Great Awakenings, the audiences were mainly skeptical, if not downright hostile, toward Christianity. If anything, they ridiculed the manifestations, and individuals were shocked to find the manifestation happening to them. By contrast, what you see today in many Christian events is large groups of professing Christians, not skeptics, having a Christian good time. There's not necessarily anything wrong with this; emotion is good. It's just that we should not equate revival with emotional responses.

Second, the results were different. In the Great Awakenings, hundreds of thousands of lost people were saved, truly converted to the Savior. When the revival type meetings ended, whole towns were radically transformed. These were the truest manifestations of revival. Families were reunited, saloons went out of business, houses of prostitution shut their doors, and you could hardly walk down the street without hearing hymns sung from the homes. In contrast, when today's "revival" preachers leave town, the cities are hardly changed at all, except for a greater skepticism on the part of unbelievers. And where are the thousands of new converts? And where are the packed churches? And the changes in public morals? In so many of today's charismatic/signs-and-wonders meetings, professing Christians may be dancing in the aisles, but the onlooking world hardly notices except to laugh.

Third, the methods were different. The leaders in America's Great Awakenings sought to create *solemn* assemblies. There were no attempts to generate emotional outbursts. There was no manipulation of emotion. In fact, the pastors in the Great Awakenings worked hard to quiet people down. The weird stuff was not their agenda. A re-consecrated church, a re-evangelized community, and a re-honored God was their goal. In many of today's meetings, just the opposite is true. The whole service seems designed to rev up emotions. This has nothing to do with true revival.

Speaking of such excesses, Charles Spurgeon said,

> I had sooner risk the dangers of a tornado of religious excitement than see the air grow stagnant with dead formality.[4]

Of course Spurgeon disdained the excesses and counterfeits, but that did not cause him to reject all "enthusiasms" — his word for manifestations — as counterfeit.

> I am glad of any signs of life, even if they should be feverish and transient, and I am slow to judge any well-intentioned movement; but yet I am very fearful that many so-called 'revivals' have in the long run wrought more harm than good. Places which have had the most of religious excitement are frequently the most hard to reach... But if I would nail down counterfeits upon the counter, I do not therefore undervalue true gold. Far from it. It is to be desired beyond measure that the Lord would send a real and lasting revival of spiritual life."[5]

Writing of Camp Meetings led by Rev. Barton Stone, Erwin Lutzer says,

Between 10,000 and 25,000 came with wagons, carriages, and by foot. People fell down, crying out, trembling, and not infrequently "sinners dropping down on every hand, shrieking, groaning, crying for mercy, convulsed; professors [i.e.,those who profess to be saved] praying, agonizing, fainting, falling down in distress, for sinners or in raptures of joy! Some of these extremes were often used by critics to discredit the meetings. However, undeniably God was at work.[6]

All of which is to say this: in revival, God can and may do strange and wondrous things to people; sometimes he overwhelms them with his presence. *But these manifestations are never the issue.* What counts is God so transforming his church that large numbers of unsaved people flock to Christ, all out of proportion to our efforts. Without that, it might be exciting, or moving, or spiritual, but it's not a revival.

Peter Cartwright lived well into his nineties, long enough to watch the wilderness become settled. He preached over 14,600 sermons and personally saw over ten thousand conversions to Christ. He contributed greatly to the salvation of the American west, helped launch a worldwide missionary movement, and built hundreds of churches.

The condition of the church and of society most often go hand in hand. As goes the church, so goes the world. The genuine revival of the church catalyzes the healing of society.

Once again, the Second Great Awakening faded, and churches began a downward slide.

THE THIRD GREAT AWAKENING, 1857-1858

The Third Great Awakening is often called the Quiet Revival or the Laymen's Revival. It lasted only two years, from 1857-1858. Once again, American Christianity was on the downhill slide. There had been flare ups of revival in Canada, Ohio, and the West. In Pittsburgh, two hundred pastors gathered to pray for revival. But this revival really took off from unlikely begin-nings. In 1857, the financial markets collapsed. Banks folded. Railroads went out of business. The monetary system was on the brink of collapse. Jobs were scarce, and the average working American faced tremendous pressure.

A young man named Jeremiah Lanphier launched a prayer meeting in New York City in the basement of a church. His pastor was out of town, and Lanphier thought he would approve. His purpose was simply to seek God's mercy in the midst of the financial crisis.

Jeremiah Lanphier sent out invitations to pray on September 23, 1857, at noon. On that day, Lanphier found himself alone. Finally, at 12:30, five people trickled in. The next week, the meeting grew to twenty, and then to forty. All of this, led by lay people. It was decided to hold prayer meetings every day. Soon, the room was packed, and a second room in the church was used. Gradually the meeting outgrew the church and went into a theater that could seat three thousand. By March, 1858, that prayer meeting was packed.

By April, countless theaters, churches, printers' shops, fire stations, and police stations were opened up for noon hour prayer meetings. They all followed the same form, with laypeople leading, and taking turns praying. There were no manifestations to speak of, just hearts of believers from all denominations melted together in prayer. The prayer meetings spread up and down the Atlantic. In Boston, Philadelphia, New York, and elsewhere. All endorsed by ministers, but led by laypeople. God was doing something remarkable within the church. And what happened outside the church?

Conversions were soon reported. As a result of these packed out prayer meetings, churches were crowded and souls were saved. It is estimated that in New York alone, upwards of 50,000 people came to Christ. J. Edwin Orr notes,

> The phenomenon of packed churches and startling conversions was noted everywhere.... "from Texas, in the

South, to the extreme of our Western boundaries, and our Eastern limits; their influence is felt by every denomination." [The revival] first captured the great cities, but it was also spread through every town and village and country hamlet. It swamped schools and colleges. It affected all classes without respect to condition. There was no fanaticism... It seemed to many that the fruits of Pentecost had been repeated a thousandfold. At any rate, the number of conversions reported soon reached the total of fifty thousand weekly, a figure borne out by the fact that church statistics show an average of ten thousand additions to church membership weekly for the period of two years.[7]

IT HAS BEEN A LONG, LONG TIME

That was a century and a half ago, and there has been no national revival in America since then.

The great evangelist Charles Finney suggested revival was the predictable outcome of certain steps the church could take. Like many others, I disagree. Revival cannot be manufactured, created, or predicted. It is a sovereign work of God in his own place and his own time. We cannot schedule one, or, God forbid, make one happen.

But we can ask.

We can pray and seek.

We can lay again the foundation of Reformation doctrines, so that revival has something solid to stand on.

There is absolutely no way that human power or ingenuity or strategizing or planning could accomplish it. Only God. He has the power. The central doctrinal truth of revival is this: God is the absolute monarch of the human heart. And in revival, he turns hearts *en masse* to himself.

My goal has been to first create a conception of revival, and then to stir your heart to pray for revival. Only this can rescue us from the chaos engulfing our world.

America's Great Awakenings were all different. The First

Great Awakening used scholars like Edwards and Whitefield. It was emotional without being fantastic. The Second featured rough and tumble circuit riders like Peter Cartwright. It was both emotional and fantastic. The Third was led by lay leaders, beginning with Jeremiah Lanphier. It was neither emotional nor fantastic.

In each case, God did what he saw fit. God was sovereign. God was in charge. God took over. And he used all sorts of people to serve his will — educated, uneducated, articulate, stammering, young and old. All the plans and efforts of the churches receded into the background. God is full of surprises, and you can neither confine him nor tame him. God becomes all in all.

Can we create revival? Absolutely not. But we can be ready for it, and we can pray for it, and we can ask God for it.

Let us pray.

O LORD, I have heard your speech and was afraid; O LORD, revive Your work in the midst of the years! In the midst of the years make it known; In wrath remember mercy. (Habakkuk 3:2)

Until then, we are to be faithful in the ordinary days, praying for the day when "the earth shall be filled with the knowledge of the glory of the LORD, as the waters cover the sea."

1. Dowley, T. *Introduction to the History of Christianity*, pp. 438-439.
2. *Edwards,* A Faithful Narrative of the Surprising Work of God.
3. Gardiner Spring in Ian Murray, *Revival*, p. 118.
4. As quoted in Eric W. Hayden, *Spurgeon on Revival* (Grand Rapids, Zondervan, 1962) p. 79 from *An All-Around Ministry*, p. 181.
5. Hayden, pp. 79,80 from The Sword and the Trowel, 1885, p. 514.
6. Erwin Lutzer. *Will America Be Given another Chance?*(Chicago, Moody Press, 1993), p. 16.
7. Orr, in Hardiman, pp. 188,9.

Oh, that You would rend the heavens! That You would
come 'down! That the mountains might shake at Your
presence! (Isaiah 64:1)

OUR SPACE-TIME UNIVERSE is held together by a spiritual
universe at its core. In that spiritual realm, Scripture reveals the
existence of an epic battle. The battle rages between good and
evil, light and darkness, God and the devil, angels and demons.

That fierce battle in the invisible supernatural realm spills
over into our visible natural realm every single day.

Revival remains one of the mightiest weapons in God's
arsenal.

Since there has been no nationwide American revival in
about a century and a half, our institutional memory of the
subject is understandably dim.

Perhaps I can shed a little light on it with a first hand
description.

This is taken from the journal of an uneducated farmer
named Nathan Cole. Cole describes his reaction upon hearing
that George Whitefield would soon be preaching. It's a long
quote, but really gives you an idea of the intensity of revival.
[Spelling and grammar remain largely uncorrected.]

Now it pleased God to send Mr Whitefield into this land. I longed to see and hear him... and then one morning all on a sudden there came a messenger and said mr whitefield is to preach at Middletown this morning at 10 o'clock.

I was in my field at work. I dropt my tool that i had in my hand and run home and throu my house and bade my wife to get ready quick to go and hear mr whitefield preach... and run to my pasture for my horse with all my might fearing i should be too late to hear him and took up my wife and went forward as fast as I thought the horse could bear and when my horse began to be out of breath i would get down and put my wife on the saddel and bid her ride as fast as she could and not stop or slack for me except i bade her, and so i would run until I was almost out of breath and then mount my horse again... fearing we should be too late to hear the sermon for we had twelve miles to ride dubble in little more than an hour.

i saw before me a cloud or fog i first thought of from the great river but as i came nearer the road i heard a noise something like a low rumbling thunder and i presently found out it was the rumbling of horses feet coming down the road and this Cloud was a Cloud of dust made by the running of horses feet. It arose some rods into the air over the tops of the hills and trees and when i came within about twenty rods of the road i could see men and horses slipping along - it was more like a steady streem of horses and their riders scarecely a horse more than his length behind another -- i found a vacance between two horses to slip in my horse and my wife said law our cloaths will be all spoiled see how they look ["Lord, our clothes..."] - and when we gat down to the old meeting house thare was a great multitude it was said to be 3 or 4000 and when i looked towards the great river i see the fery boats running swift forward and backward - when i see mr whitefield come up upon the scaffold he looked almost angellical a young slim slender youth before thousands of people and with a bold undainted countenance and my hearing how god was with him everywhere as he came along it solemnized my mind and put me in a trembling fear before he began to prach for he looked as if he was Clothed with authority from the great god and a sweet solemnity sat upon his brow and my hearing him preach gave me a heart wound and by god's blessing my old foundation was broken up and i see my righteousness would not save me.[1]

This is what happens in times of revival. Satan can't hold back the flood of interest in the gospel of Christ. Unusual crowds, displaying divine intensity, rush to salvation, and the consequence is a radically transformed culture.

The burden of this book is that our culture has passed a tipping point. We have lurched into the land of godlessness. I lay much of this cultural rot at the feet of the church. I don't think anyone or anything can fix us, apart from the power of God in revival.

When God reawakens the church, he breaks through the hardness of heart that rationalizes a life with God on the periphery. He points to sins embraced and excused, and he brings about repentance. He convicts of broken relationships, bitterness, vengeance, racism, sexism, greed — all the sins that push people apart and damage a world already in trouble.

In revival, God reawakens the Christian conscience. He fast-tracks the divine purposes of grace-inspired repentance, grace-powered holiness, reconciliation, and restoration. Revival starts here, in the church.

But it isn't revival until lots and lots of people are getting saved. Yes, God first awakens his church, but revival doesn't stop there. Revival impacts the world.

I am suggesting that revival is our only hope to counteract the levels of chaos we see.

America's three Great Awakenings...

- Planted the seeds to eventually abolish slavery

- Turned addicts and alcoholics into faithful fathers and mothers
- Strengthened families
- Ushered in child labor laws
- Emptied out the saloons
- Emptied out the brothels
- Instilled a work ethic into society
- And on and on

Biblical Christianity created the kindest, most generous, most life-affirming culture history has known, despite its many imperfections.

Revivals set America on a biblical and Christian foundation, and that foundation created the most free and affluent nation in the history of the world.

The more we turn our backs on our Christian foundation, the faster we will race downhill toward a societal cliff.

In this chapter, I'd like to think through some theological issues around the topic of revival.

WHAT CAUSES REVIVAL?

There has been a long-running tug of war over what causes revival.

In the 1800s, an evangelist named Charles Finney burst on the scene. Finney is the preacher who paved the way for evangelists a century later like D.L. Moody, Billy Sunday, and even Billy Graham.

Finney was trained as a lawyer, so when he preached, he knew how to make his case. Together with several other evangelical leaders, his religious views led him to promote social reforms, such as anti-slavery and equal education for women and African Americans. He was president of a college which accepted students without regard to race or sex. Under his leadership, the faculty and students were activists for abolition of slavery, for the Underground Railroad, and for universal education.

In 1935, Finney published his very influential *Lectures on Revivals of Religion*.

Finney presented a controversial view of revival. He said that revival is the predictable outcome of the church taking predictable steps. If Christians do xyz, God sends down revival. He writes,

> You see why you have not a revival. It is only because you do not want one. Because you are neither praying for it, nor feeling anxious for it, nor putting forth efforts for it. I appeal to your own consciences: Are you making these efforts now, to promote a revival?

Finney's views represented a radical change in the understanding of revival. His views are called *revivalism*, which is not the same as *revival*.

Finney argued that revival comes through the consecration and prayers of the church. He maintained that revival was the predictable outcome of certain steps that Christians can take. By inference, he argued, if there is no revival, it is because God's own people are not taking the required steps.

That was a major shift in thinking.

Before Finney, revivals were largely understood as the sovereign work of God. Only God could decide when and where to send a revival. We could and should pray and prepare and consecrate, but, in the end, it is always God's choice.

One author describes the earlier view, and in my theology, the correct view, like this:

> Therefore, they preached the gospel, pleaded with sinners, and prayed for fruit like they had for years; and for reasons known only to God, he sometimes blessed these labours remarkably, and sometimes he didn't. These revivals, in other words, were

neither planned by men nor achieved by men. They did not involve any unusual or novel evangelistic techniques. They were understood, therefore, to be gifts of God.[2]

WHAT CAUSES REVIVAL?

A revival is the sovereign choice of God, given to turn around a nation, or a society in the grip of Satan's lies, and deliver them to awakened levels of faith and remarkable inflow of new believers in Jesus.

It's God's call.
We can't manipulate it.
We can't manufacture it.
We can't schedule it.
We can't work it up.
Pray for revival? Yes.
Long for revival? Yes.
But it's God's call, not ours.
Revivals yes. Revivalism, no thank you.

WHAT IS THE CORE OF REVIVAL?

What I suggest here will be a surprise to most readers. The burden is on me to make the case biblically. The burden is on you to think about it and to decide for yourself.

Here's my thesis: *The core of Revival is the coming of Jesus in power and glory.*

Let me illustrate.

When you go to the movies, before the featured attraction starts, you will endure or enjoy twenty minutes of coming attractions.

Coming attractions are mini-previews of upcoming movies. They are supposed to make you excited about the main event.

Applied to revival, the main event is the Second Coming of Christ. That day is coming. We believe Jesus is coming again.

He is coming in clouds of glory, and his coming will be amazing.

I suggest that every revival is a mini-preview of the Second Coming of Jesus in power and glory. And, like a movie's coming attraction, revival is supposed to make you excited for the main event.

In an earlier chapter, I described what I see as the demise of interest in the Second Coming. I called it an "eschatology appendectomy."

It could be that revival tarries because the church isn't interested in the main event. Why should God show us the previews if we've already decided the movie isn't worth watching?

This tie-in between revival and the return of the Lord also explains why so many Bible verses about the second coming of Christ can do double duty as prayers for, or promises concerning revival.

- Oh, that You would rend the heavens! That You would come down! That the mountains might shake at Your presence-- (Isaiah 64:1)
- Sow for yourselves righteousness; Reap in mercy; Break up your fallow ground, For it is time to seek the LORD, Till He comes and rains righteousness on you. (Hosea 10:12)
- "And it shall come to pass afterward That I will pour out My Spirit on all flesh; Your sons and your daughters shall prophesy, Your old men shall dream dreams, Your young men shall see visions. And also on My menservants and on My maidservants I will pour out My Spirit in those days. And I will show wonders in the heavens and in the earth: Blood and fire and pillars of smoke. The sun shall be turned into darkness, And the moon into blood, Before the coming of the great and awesome day of the LORD. And it shall come to pass That whoever

calls on the name of the LORD Shall be saved."
(Joel 2:28-32)

THE DAY OF PENTECOST

Joel's prophecy makes the case for my premise.

After Jesus died and rose again, he issued final teachings to those earliest believers. Then he ascended, rising up into heaven before their sight, and waving goodbye to his tiny, fledgling church.

Fifty days later, the Jews celebrated one of their most important festivals, called the Feast of Pentecost. For this feast, Jews traveled from all over the world to come to Jerusalem. At this time, they were still scattered throughout countless nations, and though they were Jewish, they spoke countless different languages.

Early that day, about 120 believers in Jesus gathered in a small upstairs room, called the Upper Room.

All of a sudden, this happened:

And suddenly there came a sound from heaven, as of a rushing mighty wind, and it filled the whole house where they were sitting. Then there appeared to them divided tongues, as of fire, and one sat upon each of them. And they were all filled with the Holy Spirit and began to speak with other tongues [languages], as the Spirit gave them utterance. (Acts 2:2-4)

May I remind you of our definition of revival:

Revival is a sudden and intense work of God in the church so startling that it grabs the attention of the onlooking world, resulting in unusually large numbers of lost people coming to faith in Christ.

Revival starts when God does something remarkable in the

church, among his own people, among us. That is exactly what he did on the day of Pentecost.

The Holy Spirit came down with power on the early believers. This was not the first time God's people encountered the Holy Spirit, but I'll save that for another book.

They started speaking in tongues, which, in this case, means languages. These were recognizable languages the believers had never studied, never learned, and never before knew how to speak.

This work of God in the church was so startling that it grabbed the attention of the onlooking world.

> And there were dwelling in Jerusalem Jews, devout men, from every nation under heaven. And when this sound occurred, the multitude came together, and were confused, because everyone heard them speak in his own language. Then they were all amazed and marveled, saying to one another, "Look, are not all these who speak Galileans? And how is it that we hear, each in our own language in which we were born? Parthians and Medes and Elamites, those dwelling in Mesopotamia, Judea and Cappadocia, Pontus and Asia, Phrygia and Pamphylia, Egypt and the parts of Libya adjoining Cyrene, visitors from Rome, both Jews and proselytes, Cretans and Arabs--we hear them speaking in our own tongues the wonderful works of God." So they were all amazed and perplexed, saying to one another, "Whatever could this mean?" Others mocking said, "They are full of new wine." (Acts 2:5-13)

God did something to Christians that grabbed the attention of non-Christians.

Lord, send revival!

What might he do today? A miracle like a new knowledge of unstudied languages is not out of the question. Or a new spirit of sacrifice and love. Or of grace and generosity. Of holiness, empowered by grace. Of wisdom in proclaiming the gospel. Of boldness in proclaiming the gospel. Of humility and fear of the Lord. Of the church being distinctly different in our morality, purity, and love. I don't know what it will take for our generation.

But for the Acts 2 generation, the world took notice.

Peter stood up to preach.

> "But this is what was spoken by the prophet Joel: 'And it shall come to pass *in the last days*, [emphasis added] says God, That I will pour out of My Spirit on all flesh; Your sons and your daughters shall prophesy, Your young men shall see visions, Your old men shall dream dreams. (Acts 2:16, 17)

Peter goes on to quote the whole paragraph from Joel, eight centuries earlier.

Over here are Christians speaking in tongues, over there are unbelieving Jews from all across the known world, and over all of it is the outpouring of the Holy Spirit, even as Peter quotes a verse *about the last days*, about the time of the Second Coming of Christ, and saying, "this… is that…"

This is what Joel was speaking about. But wait, wasn't Joel speaking of the last days?

A revival is, at heart, a mini-preview of the coming of the Lord. And that is why the same Scriptures that speak of Christ's return also do a great job describing revival.

The most overlooked truth of Acts chapter 2, and the day of Pentecost, is that this is above all else, a revival.

The key figure in revival is not the Holy Spirit, but the Lord Jesus Christ.

We do not pray for the coming of the Spirit, as is so often seen in our churches today. We already have the fulness of God's Spirit.

Instead, we pray and work that the name of Jesus Christ would be exalted and lifted up. This is exactly what Peter preached on the day of Pentecost. He preached Christ.

The consequence was magnificent:

Then those who gladly received his word were baptized; and
that day about three thousand souls were added to them.
(Acts 2:41)

To my mind, the salvation of three thousand souls in a day
is a far greater miracle than 120 souls speaking in tongues. The
eternal consequences are of infinitely greater magnitude.

It isn't revival until unusually large numbers of lost people
come to faith in Christ. This is what happened at Pentecost.
This is the wonder of Acts 2. It is the wonder of every revival.

Imagine those 3,000 new believers, fanning out across the
globe as they returned home, telling and retelling the story of
the gospel of grace in all the tongues of Pentecost.

Please, God, send revival.

Wouldn't it be amazing to see God reach down into your
life, and my life, and our church, and our land? Wouldn't it be
amazing to live through a moment in which God did such a
work of purifying, and empowering, and emboldening that we
could not help but speak the wonderful works of his grace?

Can you imagine a church so on fire for grace and truth
that in one day, 3,000 souls are added to the family of faith...
and thousands more are influenced by their testimony?

WHAT KEEPS REVIVAL ON COURSE?

We need revival.

Lord, send revival.

But before God sends revival, he has to send something
else, or else the revival brings more shame to the name of Christ
than it brings glory.

That something else is a return to Biblical foundations, as
we discussed in our chapters on Reformation.

We live in an era when the biblical foundations of the
church have been shaken and fractured in so many ways.

- Biblical illiteracy is at an all time high among church people.
- Emotionalism.
- Activism.
- Experientialism.
- Subjectivism.
- A weird and irrational concept of tolerance.
- An increasing mash-up between Christian truth and secular error, mixed up in a stew called syncretism.
- Postmodernism, the opiate of liberal theologians, has stretched its tentacles everywhere.
- Wokeness is invading our churches and our seminaries, redefining the gospel, choking evangelism, and swamping the teaching of God's Word.

The consequence is the chaos we see in culture, and the doctrines of demons spread everywhere, like candy.

As we have seen, revival has a cousin, and that cousin is called Reformation. Once again:

Reformation is the work of God as he rebuilds the biblical foundations of the church, tears down demonic structures of deception and error, and restores the authority of Scripture and the knowledge of the gospel among his own people.

To summarize,

- Revival is somewhat emotional, Reformation intellectual.
- Revival is heat, reformation is light.
- The first urgent requirement to deliver the church from her chaotic condition is a thoroughgoing theological Reformation. We stand in desperate

need of a penitent return to the Bible and our first principles.

- Revival is like a fast flowing river. Reformation provides the banks that keep the river in check and prevent destruction.

I pray for revival.

But that revival must be founded on, and be the fruit of, a theological reformation that will hem in its excesses. I shudder to think of a revival without a reformation, especially in our loosey-goosey theological times.

OUR URGENT NEED

I see no other solution to the chaotic condition of the world today than a divine intervention in the form of reformation and revival.

I have never been part of a revival. I have never seen one. My late colleague, Paul Edwardson — a statesman-evangelist of my denomination — spoke often of some precious experiences of revival. There is a palpable work of God, unusual in impact and feel. There are tears. There is renewed consecration. Relationships are restored. Reconciliation effected. Sins renounced. Long-forgotten truths embraced. A path of spiritual growth toward maturity is embarked upon.

A new-found zeal for evangelism is born, and so many people come to Christ that the region is changed, and the change is long-lasting.

As Martyn Lloyd-Jones taught us, "The church has ordinary days and extraordinary days. Most of them are ordinary."

When the extraordinary becomes ordinary, it ceases to be extraordinary. So much for the teaching of continual revival. There's no such thing. Most days are ordinary.

In those ordinary days, we preach, we minister, we serve, we pray, we strive, and we grow. In the ordinary days, we must stay faithful.

But we can hope and pray for extraordinary seasons, because that's when a downpour of reformation and revival changes everything.

---

1. [Arnold Dallimore, George Whitefield, vol 1, p. 541].
2. Finney, *Lectures of Revival on Religion* (1835).

> But we preach Christ crucified, to the Jews a stumbling block and to the Greeks foolishness, but to those who are called, both Jews and Greeks, Christ the power of God and the wisdom of God. (1 Corinthians 1:23, 24)

PAUL SAID, "This one thing I do..." Today's church says, "These thousand things I dabble in." I cannot wrap up a book called *Chaos* without making the main thing the main thing.

In our discussion of revival, I have already hinted at the main thing.

It is time to refocus the lens of Christianity on Christ.

Christianity is Christ. Study Him. Learn of Him. Think of Him. Sit with Him. Preach Him. Hear Him. When we orbit Him, revival may come. When we orbit Him, lost people become saved. Saved people become holy. The world becomes a better place.

Proclaim Christ. Along with prayer, proclaiming Christ is how we set the stage for the Reformation and Revival we so desperately need.

The only chance we have of escaping the matrix of our well-deserved chaos is by refocusing the lens of Christianity on Christ himself. His natures. His Person. His works. His offices.

His crucifixion and resurrection, and all the attendant doctrines.

Look.

At.

Christ.

Run to the theology of our Savior. Savor Christology. Meet him in the Word, because these Scriptures, Jesus said, "testify of me" (John 5:39).

You, Christian, have been baptized into Christ. You've been plunged into him. You are one with Jesus. On the day you believed in Jesus, in that very first second of faith in Christ, the Holy Spirit of God did the biggest miracle the world has ever seen: he placed you into permanent union with Jesus Christ.

You are so joined to Christ that he is in you, and you are in him.

His status is your status.

His powers are your powers.

His privileges are your privileges.

His glories are your glories.

His throne is your throne.

His treasures are your treasures.

His riches are your riches, for, "in him are hidden all the treasures of wisdom and knowledge," and you are in him.

Look at Jesus!

He is the organizing principle of our lives and our world. The cosmic truth above every truth, the law, the word, the reality that alone can end the chaos.

In his message only, you will find forgiveness. In Christ alone you have an exalted status, royalty before God. In Christ you have an inheritance in heaven that defies description.

You have a true purpose and a reason for getting out of bed in the morning.

In Christ you have strength.

In Christ you have a friend in need.

In Christ you have an ever-present help in time of trouble.

In Christ you have a Shepherd for your soul.

In Christ you have a comforter.

In Christ you have a strengthener.

In Christ you have wisdom for living and you have confidence for dying.

In Christ you have hope in your worst moments.

In Christ you have gratitude in your best moments.

In Christ you have guidance.

In Christ you have power.

In Christ you have a shepherd.

In Christ you have a guardian of your soul.

In Christ you have authority to pray and an open invitation to come to the throne of grace *boldly* — even when you have messed up — to obtain grace and to find mercy.

In Christ you have God's own Word.

You have God's own promises.

You have God's immutable oath.

You have God's own presence by which he will safely carry you all the way home to eternal heaven and the mansion he has built for you there.

In Christ you have the complete package. You are complete in him because he is complete in himself.

How will you alleviate guilt without Jesus?

How will you atone for sin without his shed blood?

How will you have hope for tomorrow without a resurrected Savior?

What other system of religion or philosophy exalts human life as created in the image of God, and makes people special and sacred and precious to God?

There is none.

Justice cannot happen in culture unless Christ is exalted in our hearts.

Chaos is the price we pay when our gaze slips from our Savior.

What other system makes God simultaneously so infinite and glorious and transcendent, and fearsome, and at the same time so immanent, and near, and close and dear and precious as the faith of our Lord Jesus Christ?

Where else will you find the God who became human without ceasing to be God?

Where else the Redeemer, the Advocate, the Surety, and Friend?

Only Jesus says, "Come to me, and I'll pay the whole bill.

"Come to me empty handed.

"Come to me without money and without price and I will make you whole and I will connect you to God.

"Come again and again as often as you need and as often as you've strayed.

"Come to me all who are weary and heavy laden and I will give you rest."

God cleansed our sins.

God gave us a Savior.

A sinner is forgiven.

An orphan is adopted.

A lost lamb is found.

Look at Jesus.

The guilty are pardoned.

Death is defeated.

Heaven is guaranteed.

And HE is the head of all principality and power — meaning that if you take every religious leader, every idol that has ever been crafted by any worshipper's hand, every angel, every demon, every graven image, every god of every culture, of every society, of every age, and all the dark spirits and demons that animate them all — every one of those beings will bow to Jesus. He is the head. And all the principalities and powers will one day bend the knee to Jesus.

The glory is his.

The power is his.

The credit is his.

The kingdom is his.

The authority is his.

The wonder is his.

Jesus is Lord, even over the things that break your heart.

Look at Jesus!

Look at Jesus!

Look at Jesus!

How can you be in him and not be blessed?

How can you be his child and not be rich?

How can you be a Christian and not feel the overflowing, never-failing, need-meeting, soul-saving abundance of his grace?

Look at Jesus!

There's an old saying I wish we could resurrect. It's from a Scottish preacher of 150 years ago. Robert Murray M'Cheyne said: "For every look at self, take ten looks at Christ."

Look.

At.

Jesus.

He is the giant among humankind. Jesus is the gold standard. He is the one we aspire to emulate. And all that he asks of us, he will produce in us, if we keep on looking to him.

I'm not writing to make you feel guilty. I'm not writing to make you behave. I am not writing to push any program or social agenda.

I am writing to lift up Jesus Christ among the people of God, by inviting us to scour the pages of Sacred Scripture. Because if we can glimpse even a fraction of his wonder, he will draw us, he will woo us, he will attract us to the table of grace, and bid us come and dine.

No one will walk away unchanged. No one will walk away stunted.

He will fill the void in your heart.

He will bring order to the chaos within.

He will give you abundance of things that money can't buy.

He is the Shepherd of Your Soul, and you shall not lack any good thing.

You, child of God, are richer than you can possibly fathom.

And I pray that the riches of Christ will define not only your theology, but your psychology, so that you will rise above every enemy and keep the faith until you see him face to face.

It is time to grow big. It is time to stand tall. It is time to break out of the clay pot that keeps our growth root-bound and stunted. It is time to fill out the shirt sleeves of Christ, and to be mature men and women of faith. It is time to search the Scriptures. To shed dysfunctions. To be normal in our beautifully idiosyncratic ways. It is time for a lost and dying world to meet Christians who actually see Jesus in the pages of our Sacred Text.

It is time to bring the order to our private worlds, to our churches, and to our society that only comes when Christ is the sun and all things orbit him.

Jesus promised the "gates of Hell shall not prevail" against us. This is our great promise from our mighty Savior. I expect the best from Him. May we all pray big prayers to our very big Savior.

If it is true that no one ever rises above their concept of God, then we know what we need to do.

Open your Bible, please, and discover your great God, who is able to do exceedingly abundantly above all that you ask or think.

Therefore I also, after I heard of your faith in the Lord Jesus and your love for all the saints, do not cease to give thanks for you, making mention of you in my prayers: that the God of our Lord Jesus Christ, the Father of glory, may give to you the spirit of wisdom and revelation in the knowledge of Him, the eyes of your understanding being enlightened; that you may know what is the hope of His calling, what are the riches of the glory of His inheritance in the saints, and what is the exceeding greatness of His power toward us who believe, according to the working of His mighty power which He worked in Christ when He raised Him from the dead and seated Him at His right hand in the heavenly places, far above all principality and power and might and dominion, and every name that is named, not only in this age but also in that which is to come. And He put all things under His feet, and gave Him to be head over all things to the church, which is His body, the fullness of Him who fills all in all. (Ephesians 1:15-23)

If you would like to go deeper into God's Word than ever before, please consider **Veritas School of Biblical Ministry**.

- Designed for working people who want to learn the deep things of God's Word with clarity and grace.
- Make sense of theology, doctrine, and of how the Bible fits together.
- Launch your ministry for Christ and the Gospel to a higher level — no matter where or how you serve Him.
- Earn your Master of Ministry Certification without sacrificing your family, breaking the bank, or quitting your day job.
- Work at your own pace, the pressure is off.
- All the depth, all the theology, all the meaning of a seminary education, with an unshakeable commitment to the authority of Scripture and to the historic faith of evangelical Christianity.

Join our growing tribe of everyday scholars.

Find out more at...

www.veritasschool.life

Made in the USA
Middletown, DE
04 December 2020